*Find out
what is holding you back
from having the great relationship you
deserve
by taking this 5-minute quiz:*

GET THE RESPECT YOU DESERVE

7 Secrets to Getting Seen and Heard in Your Job and Relationships

by
Veronica Anderson, MD

Get the Respect You Deserve: 7 Secrets to Getting Seen and Heard in Your Job and Relationships

Rosewater Falls Inc., New York, NY, USA

Copyright © Dr. Veronica Anderson, 2022

Second edition

drveronica.com

All rights reserved. No part of this book may be reproduced in any form without permission in writing from the author, except as permitted by U.S. copyright law. Reviewers may quote brief passages in reviews.

ISBN: 978-0-9885645-1-0 (ebook)
ISBN: 978-0-9885645-0-3 (paperback)

DISCLAIMER

No part of this publication may be reproduced or transmitted in any form or by any means, mechanical or electronic, including photocopying or recording, or by any information storage and retrieval system, or transmitted by email without permission in writing from the author.

Neither the author nor the publisher assumes any responsibility for errors, omissions, or contrary interpretations of the subject matter herein. Any perceived slight of any individual or organization is purely unintentional.

Brand and product names are trademarks or registered trademarks of their respective owners.

Original cover design: Jennifer Stimson
Book design and formatting: cmgraphicshub

CONTENTS

INTRODUCTION 1
    One Little Thing to Change...4
    Self-Assessment: Be Honest 6
    Find Your 'WHO' to Get Results.......................................10
    Complete Your Tasks Today...15

WHEN DID THINGS GET THIS MESSED UP? 17

I'M SO MAD, I'M CRYING..21
    My Story...22

HOW DO I FIX THIS? 32
    What are our boundaries?...32

REFLECT AND TAKE RADICAL RESPONSIBILITY 36
    What is radical responsibility?...36
    9 Steps to Declutter Your Mind 40
    Do You Lack Personal Power? 43
    Self-Assessment: Do You Love Yourself?........................45

EVALUATE YOUR THINKING 49
    You are What You Think..53
    What exactly is negative thinking? 54
    The Power of Negativity 54
    What is Positive Thinking? 57

Affirmations to get you started 61

Reflection questions 62

SURRENDER TO YOUR SPIRIT 63

Spiritual Attraction.. 66

What else creates attraction?... 69

Your Human Design 70

Your Spiritual Fruit 83

Your Spiritual Quotient... 86

Recap... 87

PAUSE 89

What is Self-Reflection?... 95

Boost Your Self-Reflection via Journaling 98

ELEVATE YOUR ENERGY 105

Addiction to Perfection 105

Stop Caring What Other People Think 111

COMMIT TO YOUR VALUES.. 118

Boundaries 119

'I Take Care of My Needs First' Affirmation 120

Working through Your Values... 121

TRUST AND TAKE ACTION 124

How to Manifest.. 127

How to Achieve Manifestation 130

How to Quickly Get What You Want 133

HOW TO GET OUT OF THE QUICKSAND................................ 139

Obstacles to Becoming Appreciated 143

THE SECRET TO HELPING YOURSELF 149

ABOUT THE AUTHOR.. 157

INTRODUCTION

"We have met the enemy, and he is us."
—*POGO comic creator Walt Kelly*

Let's get down to business with some straight talk about respect. For whatever is going on in your life right now that makes you feel you have no respect, you haven't been able to fix it with your intellect.

You may be a smart person and can prove it to anyone anywhere any day. But respect has been elusive. You don't have it. You don't command it. No matter how hard you try, you just haven't been able to figure it out. Reading this book is one of your last-ditch efforts. Let me tell you upfront, you've made a good decision to read this book. But the question is: Will you make the better decision to take the necessary action that will get you the results you want?

You've heard of the glass ceiling. Have you heard about your ceiling of complexity? That's the point in your life where you're so overwhelmed, you're too embarrassed to approach someone to talk about anything. What happens to you when you reach this point? If you can't talk with someone who can help you get the respect you deserve, you can secretly invest a little bit of money in a book such as this to try to get this issue fixed on your own.

But let me caution you: The only way out is through, and the true secret to getting this fixed is in the who, not how.

Respect is an area that I have thought about long and hard, and the purpose of me writing this book is to cohesively put it all together for you so that you can not only understand the information but do something with it, too.

One thing I've learned from sitting with authors of books, especially from being in places like the Author Incubator with Dr. Angela Lauria, is knowing that those who've been able to get their ideas down enough to write a whole book really know their stuff. They know what they're talking about. Whenever you pick up a book, think of it like the textbooks you read in school.

What I want you to understand, while you're reading this book, is that there is a process of getting from *knowing* to *doing* to *being* that I've used on myself over several years. I have used the process on my clients in a systematic way so that they get the results in their life. Specifically, we're talking about getting you respect. Having you seen, heard, and appreciated. Owning the "don't mess with me" energy without being a bitch.

By the end of this book, I want you to be able to change your energy enough so that what happens in your life is what you really intend. Why you're not getting what you want in your life right now is because your mindset and energy is not aligned with what you say you want. How do you get from saying *you want it* to being a new person? That's what The R.E.S.P.E.C.T. Method™ is all about. That's why I wrote this book.

Let me tell you what I really want you to get. Nobody does it by themselves. Humans are meant to interact. You are meant to be in relationship with other people. You learn about life from being in relationship with other people. When you learn how to drive a car, somebody teaches you. Would you get in an airplane and fly it yourself after reading a book or blogs or watching YouTube videos? No, you would not. Unless you have a death wish. There's always someone who has to teach you.

Many authors don't talk about where they learned what they've learned. We're left to just think that these great people just did it all by themselves. But I didn't do this all by myself. I had great coaches and mentors. Some of my coaches have been Dan Sullivan, Lisa Sasevich, David Neagle, Maria Kellis, Nick Berar, Jayne Sanders, and Robin Winn. These great people have been some of my coaches throughout my journey. They have helped me see who I am and stay true to myself, and they held me accountable.

If you are anything like me, the reason you are in this pickle of being treated poorly is because of your naivete in believing that you could do it all on your own in the personal part of your life. But all the great coaches and teachers at one time or another hired greater coaches or teachers. Just like elite athletes pay to have coaches, there's usually a coach behind the coach—and *that* coach even has a coach. This is the secret. This is not the same as getting a degree. That doesn't count in this area. In fact, degrees and letters behind your name may be one of your biggest obstacles.

Before we end this section, I want to ask: Did that discussion about hiring someone to help you get to a higher level trigger you? Did your money issues get triggered by that conversation? Did you get pissed at me for telling you what happens and what the secret is? Did you get really pissed that the secret is investing in yourself, meaning you have to spend money?

Well, good! The advantage of writing this book is that I can get in your face and neither of us will get embarrassed from making a scene.

This is where we need to start it all. You need to get to the point where you understand that you deserve to invest in you. And that investment must be in the spiritual and personal growth side of your life. Being triggered might be that your money issues have been getting in the way of you moving forward. No matter how much money and income people have, rich or poor, people can still have money mindset blocks that will keep them from moving forward. Most of those ideas about money have come from your family. And in coaching, we can unravel that.

Now that I've really gotten your attention, keep reading, because one of the ways that you're going to get over being triggered is by learning The R.E.S.P.E.C.T. Method™.

ONE LITTLE THING TO CHANGE

I am going to tell you so much information in this book that will help you. The issue is you will only know it when you read it over and over again.

But to have real change, you must change your habits. We all know what those habits are. You have them when you get up in the morning and when you drive. You do so many things every single day out of habit, a repetitive action that is grooved into your brain that takes no effort at all. But you're reading this book because you are not getting a result that you want in your life.

Chances are you've been extraordinarily successful in some areas. But in another area, usually something personal, you feel like you failed, and you didn't get what you wanted or deserved. Truth be told, you have gotten exactly what you wanted and exactly what you deserve, because that is all that the universe delivers.

When I originally released the book, there was no introduction. But I started writing this after working with clients like you and watching some of the missteps they made, and recognizing the same missteps I made in my life.

One of the biggest missteps that really smart people make, especially smart women, is that they study, analyze, and overthink. If this is you, you're agreeing, shaking your head, and saying, "I know it." Because you're a perfectionist. You're thinking, "I need to read it. I need to study it. I need to memorize it." When you can spit it out verbatim, only then will you finally take action.

But that's what's holding you back from getting you the respect you deserve. Having to know something perfectly is a self-sabotage pattern that I want to quickly shake you out of.

How are we going to shake you out of this self-sabotage pattern? You're going to write down, in all the areas of your life, *one* little thing that you're doing that's not serving you.

I give this exercise to my clients. I even give it away as a freebie on my website and in emails, and tell them to do it, but I know that the people who aren't coaching with me generally aren't doing this one very simple action.

Why? Because there's no accountability. No one's really pushing them to do it. Therefore, the old sabotaging habit is not broken, and new ones are not started.

The thinking goes like this: "When I really want something, I can do it. I just have to put my mind to it and whatever it is, voilà, it's done." But, if it were that simple to get seen, heard, and appreciated in the areas of your life that really matter to you right now, you wouldn't have bought this book.

There's a secret about this *one* little thing I'm asking you to do. After you read this introduction, I want you to write down that one tiny action and then go do it. The secret is not just knowing but *doing*. Doing will turn you into *being*. Being means you have formed a new habit, and it's finally integrated into the real you.

The goal of this book is not for you to just *know* how to get respect, but for you to learn how to *do* the actions to *be* respected. There's a reason I said upfront that you need a mentor or a coach on your team, somebody to whom you have actually paid money to help you, guide you, and hold you accountable, so you can rise to your greatness, to persist through the obstacles and fear.

Why is this important? As my coach, Lisa Sasevich, has said at events, "When people pay, they pay attention!" It's important to make people pay significantly enough so that whatever they are working on will stay a priority, at top of mind. Enough money at stake tends to hold one's attention.

For instance, when it comes to investing in myself, I don't pay close attention to anything unless it's at least $10,000. That's my Mendoza Line. If it's not $10,000, I might not do it. Now, truth be told, I've paid more than $10,000 for some coaching services and not done the program. I had ghosted the program, but really, I ghosted myself! I'd created a self-sabotage pattern and not done what I've paid more money for. Can you believe that?

It's not that I won't do anything absolutely all the time, but if I spend a hundred or a thousand dollars, it's likely that I'm going to have an easy time ignoring whatever service I bought. If it's $10,000, I start to pay attention. When it's $20,000, $30,000, $50,000, or $100,000, I'm really on board. To be clear, this is not about buying material things, but for my own growth and development.

I want to let you know this because I want you to eliminate the excuse that you tried this before, that you didn't do it, that it didn't "work."

SELF-ASSESSMENT: BE HONEST

Here is your task for *right now*, which means as soon as you get this task. You are going to put down whatever you are doing and go do this, which will get you further in the direction of your destination.

The first activity I give my clients is the Be Honest assessment at drveronica.com/behonest. In it, you're going to be brutally honest in five areas of your life:

1. health
2. wealth
3. relationships
4. career or life purpose
5. spiritual and personal development

In each of those areas, write down *only one* thing that you are doing in that area that is not serving you, that goes against your goals, something you know you'd rather be another way.

As an example, you want to get healthier. You decide you want to drop a few pounds. What's your number one step going to be? It won't be to stop eating everything. It won't be to go to the gym. You're going to be very specific in that one area.

When Dr. Nina, one of my clients, and I went over what she was going to do in her health, we realized she was self-sabotaging by not drinking water. The one task, then, Dr. Nina committed to do was: "Every day I'm going to drink one glass of water."

For each little self-sabotaging action that you are doing, the one little thing that you can change right now needs to be practical. What can you start to do right now, in this moment? Can you go to the gym right this moment? Probably not.

Pick only one thing that you can do right this moment toward your goal. Preferably pick something for which you must get immediate results because you can't stand it anymore.

Focus on doing that *one* thing, and then do it for twenty-one days without fail. After three weeks, you can pick another task to move on to.

Why do it this way? Because twenty-one days in a row will give you a habit. You'll need a lot of brain power in the first three days to do these new tasks. They're the most challenging because you must always pay attention to what you said you're going to do.

Once you get past three days, then you're able to say, "OK, I can do this!" Once you get to a week, you're like, "I'm in the groove!" Once you get to twenty-one days, you've figured out everything; you've played all the brain games and you've managed to get there.

I'm being strict about this because oftentimes, when we make life goals, we set lofty ambitions. I do want that for you. That's part of my coaching to you. But first, we must get you doing *something*, not just writing, not just journaling.

I was following up with one of my clients recently, and she told me how she was going back to listen to our sessions. Now, on one hand, it feels good to know our sessions were so impactful that she's now realizing things she didn't get the first time around. Yes, bravo. But that's also a self-sabotage pattern! Whereas you're listening, listening, listening and writing, writing, writing. But what are you doing toward the goal?

If your goal is to get your perfect relationship, listening to podcasts is not going to get you there. Instead, figure out where you can position yourself so you'll meet new people, then decide when you're going to do it. That's going to be something. Declare some action for it soon. Put a specific time on it.

For instance, what if you want to go on a date and get a guy, but you hate online dating? (So many of my clients hate online dating, but I recommend you try it, even if you hate it.)

You need to choose how you will meet new guys. You need to change how you move through your world, because if you haven't found him already in your normal day-to-day activities, you're going to need to move around different people. You'll need to go somewhere different and do something different. You need to change your pattern.

In this self-assessment, you might consider, *what am I doing that's sabotaging myself and my relationships?* The answer is: *I'm not going out to new places to meet people.*

What can you do right now? You can go online and figure out where you can organically meet new people. You can do that maybe once a week.

This is just an idea. This may not be the right thing for you. But if you've been sabotaging yourself by staying home, whining, and complaining—as opposed to going out and doing something—it's going to be hard for you to go out and do things. It's safe for you now to stay in because there's no fear of rejection.

Even during the height of the COVID-19 pandemic, in the middle of a health situation where so many people got infected or died, the biggest self-sabotage pattern people had was believing "I can't go out and do things around people because it's dangerous."

I can already hear you saying, "Dr. Veronica, how can you say that?" Let me just bring this down to reality.

Most of the world is still living. About 99 percent of the world, after going through something that we've been taught to fear, is still living. Chances are you're going to continue to live when you go out. Even if you catch the bug of the times, you'll 99 percent get over it and be just fine.

Don't use anything as an excuse. How bad do you really want it? It's time to be radically honest. Go out. Start doing. Jump off the ledge. Be courageous. Expect that the universe will conspire for you because you want it so badly you are going to let *nothing* stop you.

If you find it hard to jump off the ledge, coaching can help you, because you have someone there to hold your hand. If you don't jump, coaching can help you deconstruct how to jump. When you do jump, and you hit the ground and you hurt yourself, coaching can remind you that you know how to get back up and heal.

In each of their books, Drs. David Hawkins and Joe Dispenza talk about going from knowing to being, but guess what? Between knowing and being is the matter of *doing*, and doing is a specific type of mindset that helps put you in that state of *being*.

This is why you must do *something* now. You must go from knowing to doing, and from doing to being. You could go directly from knowing to being, but that requires a major mindset change, where you're going to be doing something to get to the state of being.

Knowing means that you can spit information back out and you can tell someone about it. If you go into business school, you are learning about business, a lot of times from people who haven't done the business, so they can teach it only from theory. But I can say, as a business owner, that every day is your classroom. It's not like it's taught in school.

Doctors know that every patient is different, and they tend not to follow the textbook precisely. That's why medicine is called practicing, or an art, because every single patient is unique. This is the way they do medicine. This is the way everyone does their jobs. You take action, you see what result you get, and then you adjust.

One time, I recommended a book to Dr. Nina, and she started to read it. At our next coaching session, she said, "It's wonderful! Let me show you my notes!" That triggered in me the response, "Wow, those are beautiful notes." Nina is a brilliant woman, but she needed to break the pattern of *knowing* and get herself into *being*. My direction to her was to take one tiny principle from that book, identify the one piece that she could put in her life immediately, and begin to do it.

Remember, it's important to stop analyzing and overthinking and start doing, so that you can *be*. This is important because to get a different result in your life, you have to *be* the person that is living that result.

If you want to be in a relationship, that means you must *be* in that particular state, so that it comes to you. You must be that person. This is how everything in the universe is produced.

FIND YOUR 'WHO' TO GET RESULTS

As I write this introduction, I have beside me many of the books that have gotten me through tough points in my life: *Dark Nights of the Soul*, *When Things Fall Apart*, *Think and Grow Rich*, and *The Four Agreements*. These books have really made an impact on me. But what has made even more of an impact is having coaches and teachers to help me figure out how to put these ideas into my life, so that they made a different me.

As you read this book, plan on reading it at least three times. Number one goal is to *know* and understand The R.E.S.P.E.C.T.

Method, which I use to coach my clients to get results. By the end of your first reading, you'll have read about what The R.E.S.P.E.C.T. Method is, but you may not be able to say it back. I help smart women get what they want in their relationships using The R.E.S.P.E.C.T. Method.

On your second reading of this book, ask yourself: How do I actually do these things? That's where it becomes a little bit harder. That's why you're going to need some type of coach or teacher to help you.

One of my coaches, Dan Sullivan, came out with another book, *Who Not How*, in 2021. (He writes at least one book per quarter each year.) I've been coaching with him the last five years. He has always talked about identifying the who, not figuring out the how. It took me a while to realize that any time I have any type of issue in my life, I must figure out *who* can help me, and stop trying to figure out *how* to solve the problem myself. How I solve the problem is to look for a who—someone who can get me there faster, who knows the information, and then follow what that *who* (the coach, mentor, or other vendor) says. They know how to get the results you want to get, so follow their directions. When you get lost, go back to them and ask for more directions.

When I wanted to figure out how to write a book in a certain style, so that you would read it and get results, I enrolled with Dr. Angela Lauria's Author Incubator.

When I wanted to understand how to find more women like the clients in this book, so I can help them get the same results as my clients did (as you'll read about them in this book), I asked myself, where do I find more of these people who need my help? I joined Ask Method Coaching with Ryan Levesque and created a quiz funnel.

When I wanted to determine how to get this book into your hands, I joined Mike Shreeve's Peaceful Profits program.

When I wanted to know how to put the principle from *The Four Agreements* and *Think and Grow Rich* into actions so that I would get the results like those books, I enrolled in David Neagle's The Elite Mind group (which, incidentally, is where I became friends with Stanley Dankoski, the editor of the very book you are reading and one of two people who recommended I check out Peaceful Profits).

I have found a *who* for every step of the way. When I was in a dark night of the soul, I found a psychologist, Dr. Melinda Contreras Byrd.

When I wanted to learn how to craft an effective webinar, I joined Lisa Sasevich's Sales Success and Authenticity Mastermind.

When I wanted to learn how to have a self-managing business, I joined strategic coach Dan Sullivan's program.

I've been in many of these programs for years.

Am I in spiritual programs? If you've read my book, *Too Smart to Be Struggling*, you'll understand that I've had spiritual coaches. My favorite spiritual coach is Nick Berar, aka "I have no letters behind my name." When I first went in, I had no idea what I was paying him his $8,000 fee for, but I knew it was going to be good. I trusted I was taking the right steps.

My wish for you is that you decide either to hire me to guide you on how to fast-track getting respect or to hire another coach or teacher that you know will help you be seen, heard, and appreciated in the way that you deserve. Hire at a high level and show the universe energetically that you are serious.

You get what you pay for. That's true because it shows how much you value *you*. When you invest money in your smartphone, it shows what you value. When you invest money in your house, it shows what you value. Same with your car, and your vacation, too.

It's not showing that to me. It's showing the universe. The universe will give you back what you give it. Money is energy. If you're giving your energy to material things, you may or may not get more things, but the results in your life may not necessarily make you feel good.

If you value having a wonderful business or getting your

relationships the way you'd like to have them, and if they're not yet there, you're going to have to invest energy. The two forms of energy are money and time. Where you spend your time and money demonstrates exactly what you value.

If you value you, invest money in you. That doesn't necessarily mean you're going to go down to Bergdorf and buy a nice outfit (although there's nothing wrong if you love to shop couture—I do, too). Investing in you means *you* decide who is going to be your coach.

Always, always have a coach on board. All of the high-performing athletes and CEOs have coaches, even the ones you see as naturally talented. I love basketball, so I'll share some examples in basketball. Michael Jordan had a coach. LeBron James has a coach. Steph Curry has a coach. Giannis Antetokounmpo has a coach. They're talented, but you also see that some of them—famously Michael Jordan—first overcame incredible odds through having discipline and a coach showing them how to be better. They became elite.

None of us do this on our own. People are meant for all kinds of relationships. People learn from people. But learning is not going to comprise just reading a book or just watching a YouTube video. A significant part of learning is allowing other people to show you exactly how. That's the fastest way to do it.

Think about learning to drive a car. You read up on it and pass a written test that shows you *know* it. But you're not given your license at that point. You must get into a car with a learner's permit, and next to you is someone showing you how to do it. They examine you and decide you're good enough to have a license.

Remember those first days and months when you had a license? You still felt like you didn't quite know what you were doing. But as you kept doing it over and over again, it became a habit. *Now* you can drive yourself somewhere and not even remember that you drove yourself.

The key to this driving analogy is that somebody had to teach you to get the nuances of the situation. Your specific way of learning and your specific mistakes are not the same as your sister's, your brother's, your mother's, or your father's. Every day, when you got into the car, little by little, you learned from someone else, until you were ready to go off on your own.

In a time where we can search for anything on the internet and be an expert, human learning and nature are still the same. We still learn the same through other people. But once you know something, you must do it to become proficient. Just like those awkward moments when you were so scared and you got into the car to drive your first time, you're going to feel uncomfortable doing that new thing, whatever it is.

It's important to acknowledge that growth takes place when you're uncomfortable. If you're feeling good and you don't have a little bit of uncertainty about what you're doing, not even a little bit, you're probably not growing. Therefore, I'm cautioning you to do something now because it *will* be uncomfortable. The first thing you'll do is wait and say, "I'll do it later." Self-sabotage pattern! "I'll do it later. I'm not going to listen. I'll just go through the rest of the book."

Stop. Set aside this book.

Write down, in the five areas of your life, your one action, the one little thing that you're doing that's not serving you. Then write one *tiny*, implementable action for today that you can take toward a different direction. You have to be able to start on whatever it is *today*. No matter what your schedule is, start today. To be a new person, you have to *do* something, not just know something.

Remember Dr. Nina's beautiful notebook? Some would be impressed by it. But it's a red flag. She's only tricking herself into thinking that she has changed because she has a beautiful notebook full of notes.

I asked her, "What did you do with that one little area? Tell me exactly what you did since we last talked. Did you do it every single day?"

The purpose of coaching, after all, is to keep you focused on your destination and get you back on course when you run into obstacles. Coaching guides you to get to the deep part of you and show up for yourself—so that you won't die without having realized your life purpose and without a bunch of regrets.

Dr. Nina was honest when I asked her how she was doing with her water. Was she ready to move on?

"No, I need another week," she told me. "Let's see how it goes after a week."

You must be radically honest with yourself. Are you staying with something because you need more practice and it's not a part of your habits yet? Or is it time to say, "I got that," and move on?

I want you to try this as you read through the next few chapters. Hopefully, you'll be enthralled with some of the stories you're going to read. But the true goal of this book is to help you get results.

Again, let me tell you how to get results quickly. Go to drveronica.as.me/getrespect and book an introductory session with me and my team, so that we can start your coaching as soon as possible. This is how you're going to get the quickest results in your life. It's a tried-and-true method. If you don't go to that link here, find another coach immediately.

COMPLETE YOUR TASKS TODAY

You have your two tasks for today. First, I want you to start getting results in your life, so do the Be Honest assessment. From those five areas, write down only one thing that's not serving you. Then, write one thing that you can do about it right now, today, that will move you toward a different direction and toward your goal in that particular area. Finally, go do it.

You can email me at veronica@drveronica.com and tell me what you did. I want to hear about a victory in the beginning. These little actions are going to take you a long way. I want you to celebrate. So, send me your victory. I'm volunteering to give you a coaching session, just by your booking a call, telling me that you both wrote out a Be Honest assessment and did one thing on that form for at least seven days, toward your goal.

As I write this introduction, I see in my mind's eye Dr. Nina's beautiful notebook. I'm hearing in my mind's ears Elena talking about the wonderful session that she's relistening to. And I'm thinking, do something now! Do, do, do! Because that's the only way that you're going to get results. You get results by taking inspired action. No results happen without real action.

The way to go from knowing to being is to *do*. Action is not taking notes in your journal, listening to a book, watching a YouTube video, listening to a coaching session, or going to a therapy session. Any of that is not action. Inspired action is to do something, to get out there in the world toward your goal.

So, do your Be Honest assessment and exercise, and then dive into the rest of the book. If you are ready to fast-track your results, book a call with me and my team.

1

WHEN DID THINGS GET THIS MESSED UP?

When Dr. Sydney logged on to Zoom for our first meeting, she burst into an ugly cry. I've seen this kind of scene play out many times with my clients, who are doctors and other high-performing women. The conversation moved forward into what the tears were all about.

"I'm so mad. I'm getting treated like crap at work. They don't appreciate me. I've worked so hard. I've done everything right. Whenever I ask my supervisor for something, she stabs me in my back. It's just so toxic there. I can't stand it. What am I going to do? It's not supposed to be this way. I've been trying everything. I always do the *right thing*, but it seems like nobody's on my team. I keep doing more, and I get less and less and less. I want to get into a different position, but I don't know how I'm going to have time to look for a job. How am I going to make as much money? What am I doing now? This sucks. I'm tired of having this crazy schedule. I'm tired of being underappreciated. I'm tired of not getting any respect from my superiors or my colleagues. How do I get out of this?"

I have heard many variations of this theme. Whether it be with people at work or in personal relationships with spouses and romantic partners, other family members or friends, the complaint is, "I do so much for them, and they take me for granted and treat me like crap. How do I make them change? What do I have to do so that they finally see how much I am doing for them and be grateful?"

I've also listened to this variation about relationships. Anna showed up to our first video session with a shocked and stunned expression, like she had been run over by a truck.

"I'm so upset. I'm heartbroken. I've been with him for twelve years. I've done everything to support him. He just walked out the door without warning and went with this other woman. What do I do to get him back? I can't understand it. This is just so unfair. Why did he just walk away and into the arms of another woman? We weren't even having any problems. This is just so wrong for him to treat me that way. I've done everything I can for him. I mean, even things that I didn't want to do—I've put what I wanted to the side so I could help him get what he wants. I've always been there to support him. But he's not always there to listen to me or support me. Why doesn't he appreciate all that I've done for him? If he could just understand how I feel. If he would just understand my point of view, we could fix things, because things were good."

The various frustrations I hear from the women I've coached boils down to: "I'm not being respected." This issue is such a big deal that when you go to Google and type, "How to get respect," further search suggestions are offered, with "at work," "as a manager," "from others," "from your husband," "from a man," "from your wife," and "back in your life."

This "respect" conundrum is not just something Aretha Franklin sang about. It has become an inner anthem for lots of women.

These women have worked hard in their careers. They've worked hard in their relationships. They've even put their needs aside, so that they could achieve in their career or allow their partner to achieve. And then, they realized that they felt empty, even though they followed the right path. They looked around and saw that somebody else was getting all the good stuff. Not only was someone else getting all the good stuff, someone else was getting all *their* good stuff—their job, their promotion, their spouse or partner.

What's happened? How did they get messed up like this? Why are others appreciated, and they're not? I've heard time and time again that appreciation is a fundamental desire of most people. The beauty of these stories is that there are people out there who did something about their problem. What did they do? They started by asking for help to solve the lack-of-respect issue going on in their lives.

When I visit groups on Facebook, there are constant "I don't get no respect" rants. Here's the problem with whining or ranting on Facebook—when you're whining, you're preaching to the choir. Everyone has the same problem. Only a minuscule number of people in the Facebook group choir know enough to teach you to sing your way to the R.E.S.P.E.C.T. that Aretha's singing about.

In the words of one doctor in her Facebook post:

"I decided to leave clinical medicine, which I love, because I was burned out from the lack of respect, lack of support from administrators, decrease in compensation because RVU [relative value unit] is not met, rushing through patients because we need to see thirty a day. I have other interests in many other things. I also love to do things like run, bake, travel, and have family time. I left because I had no other choice. I needed a break, needed more time with my family, and I needed to do the things that bring me peace. I loved how medicine was in the past: methodical, respected, we could take our time seeing patients and doing the right thing for them. And there was no middleman telling us to hurry because we needed to be more productive."

This is echoed repeatedly by doctors, especially women doctors, and by women in other professional positions. They feel helpless and hopeless.

Physicians can have their salary reduced, or they can be fired, if they don't meet those RVUs she was talking about. RVUs, or relative value units, are ratings physicians get by their employers. Physicians are seen as better if their RVUs are rated highly and seen as worse if rated lower. This is *very* stressful because physicians are taking care of patients to the best of their ability, and patients rate physicians on how nice they are, not having to wait a long time, and whether they fix their problem.

The recurring theme is respect (or a lack thereof). What happened that you're not getting respect? Is it because all the people out there are "bad" and "bullies?" Or is there something that you could do differently to get some respect?

By the end of this book, you are going to figure out what makes the difference between getting respect and appreciation or not. We are going to go on a journey. Together with Dr. Sydney, Anna (a college professor), and a few of my other clients, you'll learn how to make sure that you get treated right. You'll be able to take steps to change your life to get the respect and appreciation that you deserve. But the first question is: do you believe that you deserve it?

Let's get into a bit of background and then talk about what we're going to do to fix this. But first, I'm going to share some of my story of respect and appreciation. As I do, you'll begin to understand what made me start noticing the patterns relating to respect and appreciation, and how they played out in my life long before I started coaching clients in this area. I don't have any kind of immunity against disrespect myself, and I wasn't born knowing how to get it. I learned the hard way. I've done some of the same things that you have that led to me not being seen, heard, or taken seriously.

2

I'm So Mad, I'm Crying

First, I want to give you some definitions. We all hear the words "respect" and "appreciation" thrown around like salt on an icy sidewalk. What do they really mean? Let me define more specifically what I mean by "respect" and "appreciation." I decided to do what every smart woman does when she wants to know what something means: I went to the master dictionary at the University of Google.

The Google dictionary defines respect as (1) a feeling of deep admiration for someone or something elicited by their abilities, qualities, or achievements, and (2) due regard for the feelings, wishes, rights, or traditions of others.

When I cross-reference Wikipedia, it reads "Respect, also called esteem, is a positive feeling or action shown toward someone or something considered important or held in high esteem or regard. It conveys a sense of admiration for good or valuable qualities."

Now, let's define appreciation. The Google dictionary defines appreciation as recognition and enjoyment of the good qualities of someone or something.

Have you ever been mad at yourself? I have had more than one instance of being so mad at myself that it made me cry. It's not just mad either. It's a combination of anger at letting myself be taken advantage of and fear of being a fool.

My Story

I know how you feel. Let me jump back to my freshman year of college. I was nineteen years old, and I met the man who would become my first husband, on the first day of freshman week of my freshman year at Princeton University. He came walking up late with all the other hunky football players who had been let out of training camp for a few hours. He told his friend, Jim, when he saw me across the courtyard, "That's the kind of woman I want for my wife." You know how the beginning of relationships are—a whirlwind. Everything is bathed in hormones of lust, and everything is perfect, except a few minor details about him that you aren't so crazy about, but hey, you decided they were no big thing and certainly not a deal breaker. We both had strong personalities and we debated a lot. Did I mention that the sex was out of this galaxy? Good sex will make us women let go of all our respect. You know I am speaking the truth. I am brave enough to admit that, and I am not even one of those boy-crazy girls. Those damn hormones will always win.

We went off on summer break and out of nowhere, a few weeks later, he broke up with me. I called his number and found myself on the phone with his so-called ex-girlfriend from high school. She's a nice person. I know that now, but back then, she was the villain to me, and I was the villain to her. We are both composed people, so we had a conversation of pleasantries, and then he got on the phone and told me he was back with her.

What was so appealing about the girlfriend at home that he didn't see in me?

"I'm going to work hard," he said. "And I'm going to become a millionaire before I reach thirty. I need a woman, a wife, who's going to just be able to take care of me." I was so hurt because I felt that I was the perfect girlfriend. I was doing everything that I thought I should do as a girlfriend, whatever that is. Because who knows anything about anything when you're nineteen (besides having a lot of sex)? Who has any real relationship experience at that point in life?

Of course, my next task was to go about getting him back. Everything I could possibly think of as a nineteen-year-old rising sophomore. All that summer, I plotted what I would do. That summer became a blueprint of sorts to my formation as the woman I perceived would be "a good wife." Here I was, a young lady at an Ivy League school, studying how to be a wife alongside getting good enough grades in my classes to get into medical school. I ran around doing everything I thought he would want.

He never asked me to do this. He didn't demand it. I just did what, in my mind, women did to please a man so he would see her as "good wife" material. I'd write love letters and I'd say nice things and blah, blah, blah. All the stuff that we women *perceive* will make us valuable enough to get the man and keep him. You talk nice. You never get mad. And you agree with his way of being.

I was more concerned about being wife material to some guy I wanted as my boyfriend than I was about my path to being a life-saving doctor. Oh, I still had hopes and dreams of becoming a doctor, and I didn't abandon those hopes and dreams. Because my boyfriend would be proud of me when I achieved them. Men love to brag about their smart, superwoman girlfriends and wives. We are the true trophies and always have been. You might think the quintessential trophy wife is a high-fashion model with two brain cells and a nice butt; however, we smart girls know that we are the whole package, and more men value this package than let on. Smart gals always feel threatened by the beauty queens because we know that, all too many times, he'll trip into her arms. I buried whole parts of me so that I would be more attractive to him. Oh, not the Glam Girl part, though, because smiling and being hot works too damn well to get stuff from men. Only those parts that might be seen as too edgy or unacceptable. By the end of the first semester of sophomore year, I had won his affection back and would be his girlfriend again.

We dated all through college.

We got married right after college and before medical school, and we lived not-quite-happily ever after. Let me say that we had, by most measures from the outside, a successful marriage. We supported each other's visions. But his hopes, dreams, and careers were always considered primary to us. I allowed it to be that way and thought it was the right thing to do. That is what it means to be a good wife, just like the wife described in Proverbs 31 of the Bible. Things fell apart though, about twenty years after we walked down the aisle. Why? Because I wasn't true to me.

It's not so easy to see this while you're going through it. We both went off into our careers—him in investment banking, me through medical school residency and into founding and opening an ophthalmology practice from scratch, starting with zero patients. I was running around making almost a million dollars a year working part-time. What was interesting about that was that I was still second fiddle in the relationship, and he let me know I was second fiddle, because he had a more high-powered, money-making position. Oh yes, we were pulling in the dough. He pulled in a lot more. I thought that meant I had to earn my keep in other ways. It played out that, before I went to my practice, when he wanted to be taken to the train, instead of driving himself, I would drive him every morning. Then, I'd rush like a mad woman to be on time to pick him up at the night train. I would feel bad if I was late and he had to wait for me.

This is where I pause and take a breath so I can point out to you that even the stay-at-home wives and mothers did not drive their husbands back and forth to the train; however, I felt I had to do it to please my husband by being his chauffeur, in addition to running a successful medical practice, as if that wasn't enough. In my eyes, women were not valued for their professional gifts and talents. You know, we working women feel guilty that we aren't at home like the stay-at-home wives and mothers. That's because women are really good at making each other feel bad about our different life choices. The women who chose to give up their careers and stay home to run their households, without the distraction of an outside career, would make snide comments in our direction about how they made the meals and did house stuff and kid stuff. And they never invited us into their club or offered to give us a hand. In return, we working women made comments about those women who can't make it on their own and resign themselves to being the glorified maid.

Women are great at keeping ourselves divided, not admitting that the patriarchy has us all in the same boat. We women sink the boats ourselves, and then men simply go get another woman who believes that we were just bad wives and she will be so much better. Until he leaves her for yet another.

Anyway, I did everything that I possibly could do to try to manipulate my husband into believing I was someone I wasn't. I was Super Wife, with a cape and a big "S" on my chest. We went to church. We taught Sunday school. I had the babies without missing a beat. I lost no time on my career trajectory, despite birthing two sons and adopting a third. I did everything possible to have the "perfect" life, like in the magazines. Yet, I felt so damn empty. Something was missing. But I couldn't figure out what it was. I knew I was not happy. Admitting this to myself was very hard and took twenty years.

You see? You aren't the only one who is a slow learner in some areas. It took me a while to get to where I am now. It's important that you know, when you read about the solution to your "respect" problem, that you can trust that I've been there and know exactly how humiliating it feels to be a highly intelligent woman with a high-powered career, and yet still be spectacularly messed up.

I had a well-off husband, a kind and generous man. I had a great career with a wonderful practice. I had three sons who were doing well. But I still felt this deep emptiness. I fell into a severe clinical major depression. I couldn't figure out why I felt miserable because I had "everything." Cars, house, diamonds, furs, trips in first class. I knew there was something else out there that I wanted but couldn't quite put my finger on it. I had this life that looked picture-perfect.

Except I didn't feel respected or appreciated in my career or marriage. My husband would say he appreciated me. However, in any disagreement, he asserted that he was right and I was wrong 99 percent of the time. He was clear with me that his career came before my career. I don't blame him. This is the general world order we are all taught to live by, from young girls and into adulthood. Men's needs supersede women's needs. The sacrificial wife and mother are the women men admire, and his mom is always that kind of woman. Do you see now how wives and mothers-in-law are set up to compete with and sabotage each other in many circumstances? Maybe the patriarchy started it, but us women keep it going. You've seen it play out in your neighborhood, this never-explicitly-said-out-loud competition called "America's Next Top Maid-Wife," picking out who is the top maid, and the hottest sex kitten, the gourmet chef, and the always-there mother.

But I'm not angry at him for that. At the time, it didn't dawn on me that the reason he didn't see me as a truly equal partner was because I did not see myself as an equal partner. Only years later did I realize how I played perfectly into the script. Now I have the hindsight to see that, from the beginning, I put aside my wants, needs, and desires and made them secondary to his wants, needs, and desires. Of course, when I decided that it was time for my wants, needs, and desires to come first, I didn't even know exactly what they were. When I finally summoned the courage to voice what they were, I was met with hostility because I was trying to change the status quo of our relationship.

As far as my career was concerned, I had a thriving medical practice, but it wasn't quite what I wanted it to be. One of the problems with my career was that I was a doctor, in a practice that I was also running. I had no wise person beside me to guide me about life, both inside and outside of medicine. I had no direction on how to structure or craft my life or my career. A recurring issue for high-performing professionals is that people who are doing what I was doing—practicing medicine *and* running the practice—make up a small group of folks. So, how do you find coaches and mentors? Now, I know there are coaches and mentors out there. But when you're in medicine, you have no idea where to look. You're in a sea of doctors. And most of them are so competitive, they don't want to tell you how to do better. If they're not competitive, they don't have the skills or talents to tell you exactly how to make your life better. Or how to make your practice better. They don't have a protocol, they don't have a method, they don't have a system to tell you how to live your best life. And so, I became clinically depressed.

One day, I walked out of my practice and decided I was never going back. I had other doctors working for me, but I knew I wasn't coming back.

I fell into a deep-funk type of depression. I was also unhappy with my marriage. Rather than simply getting a divorce, I told my husband, "Let's separate." But before we separated, I decided that it was he who was making me feel crappy. So, I went out and got myself a boyfriend, or two or three. Along with the boyfriends, I also got a Scarlet A on my chest. Making matters worse was that, at the time, we belonged to a huge Baptist Church. In most religious organizations, there is no protocol for dealing with mental illness or marital strife, other than to throw Bible verses at you. I was treated like Jezebel. I was the adulterous wife, a Hester Prynne. The church has to abandon a woman who sleeps with a man who isn't her husband. It would be against their doctrine, even if the behavior of the woman in question was clearly a plea for help or a way out of a suicidal depression state. I think back to a woman in my church who was cast out by the other women of the church for cheating, and now, in my clear mind, I can see that she was depressed and needed therapy. Yet no one in the church had the foresight to see cheating in wives as a cry for help. It serves the narrative to simply slap the Scarlet A on her and treat these women as irredeemable sinners.

It didn't take me long to come around to the point of silently thanking my church for abandoning me. That abandonment is probably one of the best things that ever happened to me. It may sound like a cliché at the moment, but stay with this story a little longer. That tough time put me on a new trajectory of knowing and loving myself rather than some pie-in-the-sky male god that casts practically everyone into hell. I didn't realize it at the time because I was so isolated and lonely. I went on to get a divorce. I thought my "beautiful" life was pretty much over and had the fear that I would never have anything good again. I had been brainwashed just like so many others into believing that I had messed up and didn't deserve the many gifts the universe has to offer. I sat around waiting to be punished for all those "bad" deeds.

There were days when I cried. And I was surprised each day when the morning came and the sun came up. I had no idea what to do. I went to the gym, from where I had recently resigned for political reasons. But I went back because there was a personal trainer there named Dave. Dave was a wonderful man. He used to let me cry on his shoulder while I worked out. I'd go in and I'd be so depressed, I'd cry through the entire workout. I didn't really need a trainer at that time because I wasn't in bad shape. But you know why we hire personal trainers even when we are in pretty good shape? Because of that deep-down feeling that we can't seem to shake that we're not perfect enough the way we are. We're not perfect enough. I started to realize that one of the issues I was facing was feeling bad about myself. In fact, I felt bad about myself a lot. Even though I'm a doctor with an Ivy League degree, who graduated with honors, and had all kinds of other achievements in my life, I felt bad about myself. I felt bad about a stretch mark. I felt bad about being a woman, I felt bad about being black. I just felt bad about me. And I couldn't understand what to do to stop feeling so bad.

Now, this is a situation where you could end up feeling hopeless with no way out. But something in me said, "I know there's something different. I know there's a better way." Luckily, I met a wonderful psychologist who said to me, "Not so fast, you can learn something from this depression." She had me read *Dark Nights of the Soul*. And we discussed it in our therapy sessions. And she treated me without medications. Now, some people do need medication, and I'm not saying they're bad. But I chose not to take any pharmaceuticals. Instead, I went out and socialized. I took some tango classes and spent time with a good friend named Judy. I was able to come out of the depression. I didn't do it alone. I had support not only from Judy, but my other doctor friend, Alfred, who used to speak positivity to me like a prophet. The psychologist, Judy, and Alfred helped me know that I could move out of my marriage into another phase of my life, see the bright side of things, and move on.

I want you to understand that I've been there in a lot of ways. I'll tell you another secret professional women face. One of the things about being a physician is that we never feel like we know enough. That's because we're not the ones on the stage teaching. So, we keep going to get more certifications. We psyche ourselves out, believing we just need to do more research, or we need to know more of this and more of that and, somehow, we will be loved and respected.

Through the last two years, I have been in a fellowship program. Immediately upon entering the program, I thought it was a bad decision. I started to do the work, but within a few months, I was bored out of my mind. But I had thought that if I did this, and I was in with my "tribe," my colleagues, I would get respect. So, I sucked it up and kept working on this fellowship. Those two years were mind-numbing. I kept getting mad at myself because I wanted to quit. I was like, why can't I just quit this? But I had spent so much money, so I just kept going. All those games in my head kept telling me I wasn't supposed to quit.

But there was a bigger reason why I had to end up finishing it. One that I didn't see until the end. But let me tell you, I was mad at myself. After two years of mind-numbing work, I couldn't muster up the desire to show up at the graduation. I was pissed at myself because I did not respect my own wishes and feelings. I couldn't get out of my own way of feeling inadequate. I kept working at something that wasn't serving me. For two years—not serving myself—by my own choice.

I found out a month after graduation, when I finally looked at the certificate, that I graduated with honors from that fellowship. I still can't make myself feel happy about those honors. Time is precious and I am still pissed at myself for not having the courage to walk away from that fellowship and do something else that brings me joy. I think I had to go through it so that you could see, as I lead you through the steps to getting more respect, that it is always a work-in-progress.

On the surface, what was it about the situation that didn't serve? Well, I wasn't learning a whole lot from an academic perspective. I wasn't bonding with the people who were there. None of them became real friends. I stayed there doing my usual, trying to fit my square peg self into the round hole group. I spent $24,000 on tuition, plus travel and food and precious time—time that I can never get back—and for what, exactly?

Well, there is a pot of gold at the end of the rainbow.

At one point, there was racial and social unrest within the Academy of Integrative Health & Medicine, so when I reached out to its executive director, Dr. Tabatha Parker, saying, "Hey, we have to do something about all these health disparities," she reached back and said, "What should we do?"

With only four months left to go before the end of my two-year program, I realized that the universe had me stay there so that, in a huge world crisis, a new coalition could be formed because the executive director knew me and was willing to listen. I don't know if I would have been listened to if I had quit. Probably not so much. The rest of the two years, I just felt like I wasted precious time and played it small and safe.

How many things have you done that you didn't have a passion for? What are you working on now, just because you think you should? Not because you love it so, but because you think that other people will like you and be more accepting of you for doing it?

Up to this point in my newfound post-divorce life, I'd done a pretty good job of being honest and stripping away the things that I didn't like in my life. But this fellowship was one area where I attempted to keep a toe in the medical profession and be around my colleagues. The interesting part of the fellowship was that, as I was doing course work in one area, my whole life was moving in a totally different direction. The type of work I was doing professionally, in transformational coaching and intuition, was taking off, which the fellowship was not helping. I was developing my own intuition and helping people develop theirs so they could understand what their intuition is saying to them through their illnesses and their injuries and their other problems. Nothing I was doing professionally was being uplifted by the fellowship work.

Sometimes, I believe you must have these experiences, so you can tell someone else about it further down the road.

3

HOW DO I FIX THIS?

If you're anything like the rest of the world, you want respect and appreciation, and you want your good qualities to be seen and rewarded. You feel that you deserve to be rewarded for your good qualities. One thing we must realize is that before you can have other people respect and appreciate you properly, you must respect and appreciate yourself. If you don't respect and appreciate yourself, nobody else is going to respect and appreciate you.

I'm sharing my stories of respect and appreciation, and of not getting it the way I thought I should get it, because I want you to realize that I created the way I was treated. This happens in both your personal and professional life. If you think about how you're treated by your spouse, your children, your parents, your colleagues, your bosses, it comes down to what you accept and don't accept. It has to do with the boundaries you set and whether you're willing to keep to those boundaries.

WHAT ARE OUR BOUNDARIES?

Boundaries are limits and rules that we set for ourselves when relating to others. We learned most of these boundaries throughout childhood mostly by observing what was going on in our families and others. When one has healthy boundaries, they realize that they have the right to say "no." Being able to say "no" gives us integrity and self-respect.

When your life lacks boundaries, it is a set up for chaos, drama, and lots of heartache.

They didn't teach us about boundaries in elementary, middle, or high school, and not in college or medical school or any other professional school (unless you trained to be a therapist). Hardly anyone teaches us about boundaries, not even our parents. As a result, most people aren't firm in holding to their boundaries.

I was lucky to have a mother who did teach me about boundaries.

First, she taught me how I was supposed to be treated by men. How to pick the right ones who would treat me well and had similar values. She also made it clear, in no uncertain terms, that I should not let them talk to me in abusive ways, and if they ever hit me, there was no second chance. Good-bye for good. One strike and you are out. I thank my mother for her very high standards, which she learned from the lady that raised her, her adoptive mother.

When I told you a story about my first marriage, you probably thought, "Oh, my God, he was a horrible guy." Really, he wasn't horrible. He's a nice guy who did what he could get away with because I set it up that way. I never questioned whether who he was actually worked for me. I accepted him that way and didn't push back until more than twenty years later. I wanted to make it work for me even when it didn't work for me. Just like you, being human makes me do everything I can to be loved and accepted to keep from being alone.

We're all afraid of being alone at our core, afraid of being abandoned. Our desire to be loved and to belong to some group, whether it be in a job, profession, family, friends, or romantic relationships and marriage, leads us to cross our boundaries and invite others to do so, even though we know that, deep inside, we would like something different. Humans thrive on relationships. We consider it a deep need like food, air, and water.

One sentinel life lesson I've learned from attending the School of Hard Knocks, and from coaching my clients through similar circumstances, is that when you don't allow your boundaries to be easily broken, and when you are exactly who you desire to be—the true you—more opportunities, more love, more appreciation, and more respect appear in your life.

When you let down your guard and open wide the gate to your boundaries, you risk respect and appreciation. What is real in getting what you want—being seen and heard—is to be strong and resolute about what will and will not work for you, and being courageous enough to act and have faith that life will go your way.

While reading this book, you will be taught a process to get respect and appreciation through The R.E.S.P.E.C.T. Method that I discovered and use with my clients.

First, you'll reflect on when the issue of not being respected started. You will be taught some effective exercises to quickly identify and clear your fears. The emotion of fear is indicative of not living in the present moment, but rather focusing on the past or the future. Fear is based on worrying about something that has happened in the past, that may happen now, or that could happen in the future. In this exact moment, you are fine. How do you know that? Because you are sitting reading these words.

We will walk through setting and keeping boundaries.

You'll also learn how to fiercely trust the process of change. You will be able to embrace that the universe will meet you exactly and precisely where you are and take you by the hand and lead you forward.

Finally, you will discover the key to the entire process is ongoing guidance and accountability by master mentors to help you quickly overcome obstacles. Part of what you will learn here is how to identify the right guide to help you master the "how" of each step.

Here are the seven steps of The R.E.S.P.E.C.T. Method™:

R: Reflect and take radical responsibility

E: Evaluate your life and your strengths

S: Surrender to your spirit

P: Pause now and release judgment

E: Elevate your energy

C: Commit to your boundaries and values

T: Trust and take action

I'll cover each of these seven steps in its own chapter. During your journey through these steps, you will follow the journeys of my clients—Dr. Sydney, Anna, and others—so you can see how situations play out in real life, and how using the method can move you away from being disrespected.

By the end of the book, you will know the step-by-step process to take back your respect, how to get appreciation, how to let go of your fear, and how to move forward and get what you want in your career and in your relationships.

Let's get going.

4

REFLECT AND TAKE RADICAL RESPONSIBILITY

What does it mean to reflect? Think of yourself standing in front of a mirror. When you look in the mirror, you see *you*. You can see *all of you*. You can see the parts that you like about you, and the parts that you don't quite like.

Some people see only the stuff they don't like about themselves. We're going to talk about not doing that in the future. You've got to learn how to be gentle with yourself. Reflecting is about taking radical responsibility.

WHAT IS RADICAL RESPONSIBILITY?

You have created your life. Until now, you have made the choices that resulted in your path happening the way it happened. Most people reading these words have had a free life, aside from childhood when your parents made decisions for you. You became an adult, and you continue today to make decisions. Some of us look at our parents and blame them for how our lives have turned out. Are you able to let go of what your parents did? Are you able to forgive your parents? Are you able to realize that being a parent is really hard?

Now is the time to take responsibility for how your life turned out, since you're the one who has been at the steering wheel of your life all along.

When Dr. Sydney started working with me, she was in a pickle. She didn't like her position in the hospital clinic. She wasn't on great terms with her supervisor, who disregarded her suggestions. She was unable to see how some of the situations that were happening in her work environment were situations she herself had created. This is the time to think about how you have reacted in certain situations.

When Dr. Sydney first went into the hospital practice, she seemed to love what she did, but certain things weren't quite right. In fact, she was in a traditional allopathic environment. Although she had the typical Western training, her thought process was natural and holistic, and that's the approach she wanted to do.

First, it was about selecting a practice setting that would fit more with her values. As she started to run into issues, it was easy to see why. The environment she was in was a traditional medical environment, focused on prescribing drugs to patch up illnesses. What she wanted instead was a more holistic practice, focused on the total person. She wanted to introduce lifestyle modifications like healthy eating, exercise, mind-body stress reduction techniques, and the utilization of vitamins, botanicals, and other complementary ways to get well and stay well.

Dr. Sydney's position in a big hospital setting was a far cry from the holistic treatment she wanted to use to help her patients. We all have the illusion that we'll go into a job or situation and change things to our liking.

However, it's extremely difficult to change a situation such as a job when that's not why you were hired. They hired you based on what they wanted for the position. Unless that job description has "change agent" as one of your tasks, the human resources department isn't expecting you to change anything, so it's going to make it difficult for you to change what's going on in the work environment around you. When you accept a position, unless you are being hired into the C-Suite to affect change, you are generally a cog in the wheel.

Think about and reflect upon whether you experienced a situation in your work environment where you thought, "OK, this isn't quite right. But I'll accept it for now. And, as I get to know everybody, I'm going to make them see it my way."

This was how Dr. Sydney saw it when she accepted the position at the hospital. She seemed like it would be a good short-term stop, and the money was too good to just say "no" with nothing better in sight.

Reflect upon your situation in your job at this point. Look back, especially in the beginning. Were there any warning signs that it was going to be that way? Was there someone who made the hair on your neck stand up a bit, even though they were smiling and welcoming? Were there other employees who seemed to be faking that the place was fine? You probably can pick up on that and see them easily right now. Hindsight is always 20/20 and crystal clear, especially if you're truly reflecting and in the mirror. Think of choices that you made, choices that you knew weren't quite right in that position and went against your intuition. You forged ahead anyway, because your logic was that all the check marks were in the pro column for taking the position.

This isn't about absolving other people of bad behavior. This is about you taking responsibility. You chose to go into the situation voluntarily and of your own free will. You thought, "Hey, I don't have any other options, so I have to stay here for now. I'll just suck it up, things will somehow get better, and I'll get used to it." And you sucked it up, and now you're miserable. Where else does this happen a lot?

Anna, for example, might have known in the beginning of her relationship that things would turn out the way they did. What are some of the things that Anna reflected on about the relationship? She admitted she entered this relationship with an older, married man. When she met him and got into the relationship, he was not emotionally available because he was in a relationship with someone else. The typical story that many men who decide to step out of their marriage tell their *new woman* is what a horrible person his wife is or has become, how she's not meeting his needs, how they don't see eye-to-eye anymore, how they don't get along, and how they stayed in the relationship just for his kids. But now that the kids are grown, he wants to finally *get out* of his long-dead relationship.

Understand that there are warning signals when you step into a relationship. If he decided it was OK to step out of the relationship, be unfaithful to his wife, and treat her that way, you need to understand that this could happen to you, too. You have to look hard in the mirror. Take responsibility that you decided to enter the relationship knowingly and freely, despite what the other person was doing.

Reflect upon what happened in a relationship, on how those seeds, sown at the beginning, turned out not quite the way you wanted it. The typical conceit of the *other woman*, for example, is that she is somehow better than the wife or the current girlfriend. The *other* woman decided that she was good and the previous women he was with were bad. What's the truth?

When you can get honest about how life and relationships go, there's no villain here. The current wife or ex-wife is not a villain. You are not a villain. When he walks away from you, the same way he did to his ex-wife or ex-girlfriend, he's not a villain either, at that point. There are consequences that may take years to play out, when you decide to choose a relationship with a man that wasn't truly available physically or emotionally.

There are lots of relationships that begin this way. Perhaps you are in one of these relationships now, where you slipped onto the scene while he was still officially with his last girlfriend or married to someone else. Since you wanted something different and he was oh-so charming, you ignored the red flags and compromised your values, justifying to yourself why it would be fine and everything would go your way. That huge compromise usually ends up coloring the entire relationship. When you compromise in the beginning, you end up compromising the entire relationship. Then, you believe that, because you've made those sacrifices, he should do exactly what you want him to do. The reality is that each person in an adult relationship has a spiritual journey going on and has the right to live their destiny. Scary but true, which means that every day, based on our needs, we make the choice whether to stay or go.

The first phase of the reflection process is for you to step back and figure out exactly where you are. How do you feel about you in relation to the rest of the world? Where are you on your scale of personal power?

I'll unpack personal power more in a moment, but for now, know this: If you find you've let go of your personal power, it's likely you don't respect yourself. You must respect yourself. The more you choose to understand and embrace your personal power, you'll find you can get more of it, which will cause you to gain respect and appreciation.

9 Steps to Declutter Your Mind

But before you reflect on your relationships, we need to review nine tips to declutter your mind.

1. Focus on your physical clutter

Look around you and decide to clean up and clean out. You may be a person who can work in a lot of clutter, but it's a sign of disarray when you have lots of clutter around you. Physical clutter negatively impacts your mental clarity. You may want to find a space where you can declutter.

Caution is key at this moment. One of the most common ways to distract yourself or procrastinate from doing the necessary inner tasks at hand is to take on other tasks in your home or outside the home, such as volunteering. Identify if this is you.

Would you rather clean out your closet than examine the extra clutter in your head? Pick a day and take one area that you can make your own to declutter. You are not allowed to use more than one day to do this task. Period. Pick the date on your calendar, and whatever you get done that day, that's it. No major redecorating or anything else to avoid what you know you need to do.

2. *Write it down.*

Grab the yellow pad. You don't need a fancy journal or anything else. Just the act of writing things down will help you declutter your mind. When you think of something that irritates you or bothers you, get out your pad and write it down. This will allow for reflection later.

3. *Let go of the past.*

A mind full of past regrets or old grudges is likely cluttered. I know it's easier said than done. But remember the past is just that—the past. Try to leave it there when you can. When you free yourself from fretting about the past, you naturally invite more clarity into your present.

4. *Avoid multitasking.*

Yeah, I know. They say women especially can multitask, but it's not true. You need to focus on one thing at a time. Just as I'm sitting here writing this book, the only thing I can do right now is sit here and write this book. And when I take my attention away from it, it takes me longer to do it. I would never suggest that you make any snap decisions. The ability to multitask is often considered a strength. It isn't a strength at all. The funny thing is that too much multitasking often leads to a lack of focus on any one thing. It is also horrible for your cluttered mind. You can focus with clarity when you are doing one thing. How can you focus with any clarity when you're doing five things at once?

5. *Make confident decisions.*

You do need to be confident in your decision-making skills. If you're the type of person who shies away from making decisions, eventually you will find your mind becomes cluttered with all those unresolved issues. Make a decision to get the clutter out of your head.

6. Talk it out.

Do you have something on your mind that is taking up a lot of your energy or focus? Talk it out. You can even turn on your phone recorder and talk.

If it's an issue with someone else, you can talk it out with them. Don't waste time complaining to a random person who isn't the person you have the problem with.

If that is not an option, pick a good friend who's a great listener and talk with them. Don't pick the kind of person who won't listen or just wants to solve the problem to get it off their plate. They are well-meaning and feel they are helping you. But, many times, this is about you thinking out loud with someone who can sit quietly and only speak when you ask them to do so. Talking it out will help you come to a decision.

A person who can listen without defaulting to being a problem solver is the best type of sounding board. If you're having trouble making any kind of decisions, go out for coffee and chat with a confidante who's willing to sit there and listen.

7. Walk it out.

Another great way to clear your mind is to take a walk. Ideally, you can find some place quiet. It doesn't have to be a long walk; even a stroll on your lunch break can help. A calm, peaceful walk is a great way to let those clutter thoughts drift away.

8. Control your social media intake.

Yes, we are living in the digital age, but you must control your media intake completely. We're inundated with updates from loved ones, old school friends, and past acquaintances via social media. It can be a lot to take in. Try limiting social media, regular media, and texting. You don't have to quit cold turkey; just check these things less often. Put yourself on a schedule. Set a plan to check it at 8 a.m. and at 6 p.m. That's it. You will quickly discover that your mind is less likely to be filled with pointless and cluttering thoughts about other people's lives.

9. Get better sleep.

I think by now we all know the many benefits of sleep. But did you know how vital it is to your mental clarity? According to research, a lack of sleep deprives your brain cells of their ability to connect. This lack of cellular communication can cause confusion and mental lapses—hallmarks of an over-cluttered mind. Before you go on to reflecting, start by decluttering your mind.

DO YOU LACK PERSONAL POWER?

These days, the word *empowerment* is thrown around quite often. But how do you know whether you have it or not? Lack of personal power translates to lack of respect. Experiencing emotions like hate and frustration stem from feeling unempowered. When you feel like you don't have control over certain aspects of your life, it's difficult to maintain control over your feelings. Those emotions may be a sign that you are lacking in personal power.

You can regain your personal power by changing your perception of any given situation. It could be as easy as choosing to think in a different way. When you're dealing with feelings of insecurity and frustration, your initial instinct is to try to control everything around you regardless of the situation. Take control of your personal power by choosing what you want for your life.

Here are nine signs that indicate you lack personal power. Evaluate if one or more of these nine signs are present in your life.

Sign #1. You waste your energy by complaining.

There's a huge difference between problem solving and complaining. Everyone needs a good rant every now and then. But if you spend most of your time complaining to anyone who will listen, then you're too busy focusing on the problem instead of looking for a solution. Complaining says you don't have control over the situation or your attitude.

Sign #2. You can't accept responsibility for your feelings.

If you constantly blame other people for how you're feeling, then you lack personal power. Sound familiar? You shouldn't allow the behavior of others to dictate your emotions. You can choose your emotions. Accept that you have control over your emotions, regardless of how others choose to behave.

Sign #3. You fail to establish healthy boundaries.

If you don't do this for yourself, and you often allow others to guilt-trip you into certain behavior, then you're giving your personal power away. Don't blame other people for forcing you to behave in a way you don't wish to, or for wasting your time. You're the one who allows others to take your time; you're in charge of how you establish boundaries that control how you behave and who you spend time with. And that includes professionally and personally.

Sign #4. You hold grudges.

When you hold a grudge, you are doing more harm to yourself than the other person. You waste valuable energy and time thinking about the person who wronged you. And it robs you of your ability to enjoy life. The best way to take your power back is by forgiving someone and moving on. Forgiveness doesn't mean excusing someone; it means you're letting go of the anger and hurt it caused.

Sign #5. You don't know your values.

When you don't know what values you hold, you leave yourself at risk of being caught up by someone else's values. You can be led astray down a path you don't want to take. Take your power back and acknowledge the values that are true for you.

Sign #6. You waste time on unproductive thoughts.

I bet you've spent a day wishing it was time off. Or you've spent a night wishing you were off the following day. You're wasting your time, giving the workday even more power than it should have. Take back control of your thoughts and don't waste brainpower on things that don't deserve the energy.

Sign #7. You engage in victim language.

When you say you *have* to do something or that you have *no choice*, you're turning yourself into a victim. Sure, there may be some things that are out of your control, but there are always choices to be made. And with every choice comes a consequence.

Sign #8. Your self-worth is dependent on others.

If your self-worth is dependent on the opinion of others, then you're in trouble. Your self-worth should be rooted in how you feel about yourself. You don't need to be liked by every person nor do you need everyone to agree with the choices you make or the life you lead. Never give up your personal power by allowing one opinion to determine your worth.

Sign # 9. You're afraid to stand out from the crowd.

Fear and self-doubt can be powerful, and these emotions may result in feeling desperate to blend in with your surroundings. You don't want to rock the applecart or stand out from the crowd. Trying to blend in is preventing you from being who you are. You're effectively wearing a disguise. You should be mentally strong enough to be different. Dare to stand out.

SELF-ASSESSMENT: DO YOU LOVE YOURSELF?

How much do you love yourself? Take this self-love quiz. How do you know if you love yourself? Is your self-esteem healthy or unhealthy? Self-love is something that can and should be cultivated.

There are many tools and techniques for developing it, and we'll talk about some of those in the following chapters. After all, how can you truly love others unless you love yourself first?

Part I.

Answer "yes" or "no" to each of the following questions.

1. You generally put your needs before those of others.
2. Self-care is a top priority for you.
3. You feel that you have valuable gifts to share with the world.
4. You know your worth.
5. You believe in yourself.
6. You trust your intuition and follow it.
7. You know when to say no and are OK with saying it.
8. You are glad to be you.
9. You love the life you have created for you.
10. You feel comfortable in your skin.
11. You do not depend on the opinions of others to feel good about yourself.
12. You eat well.
13. You exercise regularly.
14. You can look in the mirror and approve of what you see.
15. You are kind to yourself and others.
16. You feel compassion for yourself and others.
17. You take time for yourself to rest, relax, and rejuvenate.
18. You have a network of supportive friends.
19. You reach out for help and support when you need it and are not afraid to ask for help.
20. You have fun often.
21. You know what you want and can take steps to accomplish it.

Part II.

Answer "yes" or "no."

1. You are often self-critical.

2. You put yourself down and say unkind things to yourself.
3. You do not like what you see in the mirror.
4. You eat junk food to comfort yourself when you are down.
5. You use drink or drugs to cope.
6. You isolate yourself.
7. You are a people pleaser.
8. You put yourself last.
9. You often feel like you do not have a choice.
10. You feel a lot of resentment because you cannot say "No."
11. You feel like a failure.
12. You are afraid of making mistakes.
13. Sometimes you are too afraid to act because of what others will say.

Each "yes" answer receives one point.

Calculating your score.

Add up your score for Parts I and II. Subtract Part II score from Part I score.

If you scored between fifteen and twenty-one, then you have a healthy sense of self-worth. You love yourself and know how to look at yourself. Keep up the good work.

If you scored eight to fifteen, then there is room for some improvement. You can do much more to love yourself and bring more joy and contentment into your life. You have some good foundational practices, but you deserve more. There are many ways you can learn to love yourself more.

If you scored less than eight, then you probably have low self-esteem and low self-worth. You are much better than you realize.

Next step: if you scored below fifteen, now is the time to make some profound inner changes and love and care for yourself.

You are the most important person in your life. If you love yourself deeply, then you will have so much more to offer to those around you.

Loving yourself more will help you avoid burnout and will help you do a better job of caring for those around you. You will feel better about yourself and experience more commitment. Take action now and watch your world change for the better.

5

EVALUATE YOUR THINKING

For this section, I'm donning my physician scientist white coat, putting my hair in a bun, and throwing on my glasses. In other words, I'm going to talk to you from my professorial teaching voice because it's important for you to be able to accept that I'm not simply pulling this stuff out of my butt. There is real, good, published research behind what I'm telling you. I'm getting this out of the way here, because when we work together, we will apply these teachings so that you get results. The results are quicker when you have some background and have faith that what I suggest you do when we work together has some data to back it up.

* * *

You've reflected and realized you've made some choices that have not served you in the way you thought they would. So now you're left with the question: How do you get treated better at work and in your relationships than you have in the past?

If you want to get a different result, you must do things differently. When you think differently, you act differently and make different choices. We're going to learn how to evaluate how to think in a way that's going to lead you to different perceptions, to see situations in a different way.

Now is the time to admit that you don't quite know how to change your thinking, but we're going to deal with that right now. You must examine what you're thinking, the assumptions that you're making, and where those assumptions come from.

For Dr. Sydney, it started when she realized she wanted to do something different. She was listening to a podcast interview of a holistic celebrity doctor that she admires. In that interview, she heard this female physician sounding happy, talking about how she worked no more than five hours a day and probably about twenty hours a week. Dr. Sydney, at that moment, got mad. She couldn't understand how that physician could have such a big presence and be doing so well, in her business and financially, by only working five hours a day.

"That's not fair," Dr. Sydney said. "She's not even working hard."

Then the lightbulb went on. Dr. Sydney realized that the way she was thinking about this was due to what she was taught—that doctors should work hard in order to get well-compensated.

Dr. Sydney admitted a few realizations: Her beliefs about work and money (that you have to work "hard" for it) were tied into her own self-worth. She felt pangs of jealousy and was a bit ashamed she had those feelings. She was jealous that this celebrity doctor's twenty-hour-per-week work schedule was the work schedule she wanted for herself. She believed that this celebrity female physician, with those hours, didn't deserve to be financially successful and happy. In her long and arduous medical training, Dr. Sydney had been conditioned to a certain belief system that real doctors are supposed to do a lot of grunt work and overwork themselves—harder than hard and longer than long. Her thought pattern was that, as a physician, you're supposed to put in a lot of hours—minimum sixty a week. You're never supposed to go home early. Certainly, you're not supposed to tend to your own wants, needs, and desires before getting every bit of work done for your job.

In her mind, when you work the too-hard way, then you deserve money and celebrity. That's the life of a hardworking (and well-compensated), respectable doctor. But our Dr. Sydney didn't *have* the money and celebrity that this doctor had. She had been putting in all the long hours, not spending time with her husband, and not spending time with her child. Yet, she was getting the exact opposite of what this other celebrity doctor was getting in her life.

Can you think of a situation in your life when, like Dr. Sydney, you thought of things in a particular way that *doesn't* serve your needs? It's not your fault. You are human. You are being the A+ student in thinking the way you've been taught to think, throughout your past path in life, by family, society at large, and your education or training.

My client Anna, in her failed long-term relationship, began to shine a light on and examine her way of thinking about her expectations from romantic partners.

"If I do this for him, then he should do that for me," she said. "If I act this way, he should be able to see that I'm helping him and deserve to be seen and heard for what I want. He should appreciate that I'm helping him with his career and life. He's supposed to understand that I've made all these sacrifices for him, so he should stay in the relationship with me. I've done all the right things, so it is so unfair that he just walked out like that and went with that other woman."

As Anna went through the steps explained in this section of the book, she realized that just because she thought one way, it didn't mean that other people thought the same way. Just because she had a certain thinking pattern, it didn't mean that her boyfriend was supposed to have the same way of thinking. This important realization—that everyone has the right and free will to think the way they want—is allowed and part of what makes us all unique. It's not bad or good to think a certain way. It just is. We all have different thought processes based on our wants, needs, and desires. Anna believed that she could change his thought processes with the "logical" argument that he just needed to see how much she loved him, and how much she did for him. Once she was able to let go of some of her resentment, she was able to realize that we're all different people.

You can imagine what a tough lesson this was for Anna, given the years she had invested in the relationship. We have all had these situations where we put years into something and it falls apart. This is when we either become bitter and resentful or we learn to change the way we think in a way that makes us better. As we go through the rest of The R.E.S.P.E.C.T. Method, you will discover how changing your thinking can, many times, lead to other people changing their thinking—without arguing, browbeating, or guilting them into saying what you want to hear.

Warning: If you think you are going to learn to manipulate people, that isn't the case. I want you to understand that changing your thinking is not at all about manipulating other people. Changing your thinking is about you being the best you can be. When you're the best you can be, and you believe in you, other people in your world react differently in their attitudes and behaviors toward you. Life will seem to magically go the way you want it to go. Jobs and situations seem to somehow turn out in your favor—maybe not necessarily in the way you think it will, but in a better way. Relationships end up being the type of relationships that you want, where you are *you*, effortlessly, and they are themselves, effortlessly and naturally. The current relationship might change or fall away, and a new and better relationship might appear, one more in line with your wants, needs, and desires. Why? Because you think differently about yourself, and your energy will silently show that.

As you evaluate your thinking, reflect on the areas that have served you well. Consider also other ways of thinking that might serve you better and easier. For example, wanting a shorter work week, like the celebrity doctor who had the life Dr. Sydney wanted, doing exactly what she loved in a twenty-hour week. In coaching sessions with Dr. Sydney and Anna, we worked through questions and reflections to pivot their thinking, uncovering new and different ways of perceiving themselves and others that created what they wanted—in their career and in their relationships with romantic partners, family, and friends.

We all have a constant dialogue going on in our head about everything. We are usually either making up stories about something that happened in the past or projecting what is going to happen in the future. What does this running monologue mean for how we make choices and live our lives? Let's evaluate our thought processes and figure out some ways to change those thought processes, otherwise known as our inner monologue. Once you change how you think, you're going to think differently about you and the rest of the world, because your reality is based on what you're thinking.

YOU ARE WHAT YOU THINK

We often hear it said, "You are what you eat," but it may be more accurate to say, "You are what you think." As it turns out, our thoughts hold way more power and weight than we tend to believe. The thoughts that pass through our minds are responsible for everything that happens in our lives. Our predominant thoughts influence our behavior and attitudes and control our actions and reactions. If our thoughts are negative, those negative thoughts will inform negative attitudes and behaviors that will result in negative actions and reactions.

For instance, if you hold the belief that you are incapable of accomplishing a task or goal or simply aren't capable in general, you will align your actions and reactions in a manner that supports that belief. On the other hand, if our thoughts are positive, they will inform positive attitudes and behaviors that result in positive actions and reflections.

The key to transforming negative thoughts into positive ones, as a means of self-transformation, is first to understand, in its entirety, the negative impact that negative thinking has on our attitudes, behaviors, actions, and reactions. Then, you must understand, in its entirety, the positive impact that positive thinking has on our attitudes, behaviors, and reactions.

What exactly is negative thinking?

Negative thinking refers to a pattern of thinking negatively about yourself and your surroundings, in a way that significantly impacts the way you view yourself or the world, and that interferes with daily tasks and functioning. In other words, negative thinking gets you stuck. There are various potential causes of negative thinking which can be indicative of mental illness, such as depression, generalized anxiety disorder, and many others which are part of regular life.

The Power of Negativity

There are three leading causes of negative thoughts. First is fear of the future, second is anxiety about the present, and the third is shame about the past.

Fear of the future is characterized by uncertainty about what the future might hold. Many who have a fear of the future engage in a behavior known as "catastrophizing," or predicting the worst possible outcome, failure, or disaster.

Anxiety about the present is characterized by excessive worrying about situations or circumstances currently being experienced. Often, individuals visualize worst-case scenarios derived from a fear of losing control over the situation at hand.

It's the same with shame about the past. It is characterized by dwelling on past mistakes and failures, far more than others. This dwelling on the past limits progression and forward movement of any kind.

These leading causes of negative thinking, and others, take our minds captive and go on to shape what we believe, how we feel, and the decisions we make, given the circumstances in our life.

A prolonged period of negative thinking can result in depression, where we are more likely to get stuck in cycles of repetitive, ruminative thoughts that have a negative emotional tone. These types of thoughts can consist of judging ourselves as unworthy or unlovable, or anticipating a negative outcome of the future for ourselves. Negative ruminative cycles magnify feelings of anger, shame, or sadness, and interfere with motivation to try to move on or solve the problem at hand. The implications of negative thinking on the mind are significant. Simply thinking something negative can cause the negative thing to manifest in our lives, with no action on our part.

This was seen by researchers in San Diego, who examined the death records of nearly 30,000 Chinese Americans, and compared them to more than 400,000 randomly selected white people. As reported in *The Lancet*, researchers found that Chinese Americans die significantly earlier than would be expected, by up to five years, if they have a combination of disease and a birth year noted by Chinese astrology and Chinese medicine as ill-fated.

The research showed that the more connected Chinese Americans were to the traditional Chinese superstitions, the earlier they died. Upon review, the data revealed that the reduction in life expectancy could not be explained by genetic factors, lifestyle choices, patient behavior, the skill of doctors treating the individuals, or any other variable. Ultimately, they concluded that their Chinese beliefs were the reason behind their earlier deaths. The belief that they could die younger because they were "hexed by their stars" manifested as a shorter lifespan.

A different study, which looked at the notion of thoughts impacting physical health outcomes, found that 79 percent of medical students reported developing symptoms suggestive of the illness they were studying. The binding seemed to suggest that the constant focus on the particular illnesses they were studying led to a hyper focus on and paranoia about contracting those specific illnesses. Thus, that mindset of thinking that they would get sick created conditions within the body that allowed sickness to come to fruition.

Negative thinking can also impact the brain. A 1990 study published in the *Journal of Clinical Psychology* looked at the impact of worrying about the completion of a performance task. Participants in the study were asked to sort objects into two categories. As the difficulty of the sorting activity increased, individuals who worried demonstrated a major disruption 50 percent of the time in their ability to sort objects.

A follow-up study confirmed there was decreased performance due to increased levels of negative thoughts. Essentially, when presented with incomplete tasks, negative thinking can inhibit the ability of the brain to process information.

Another effect of negative thinking is its impact on the physical body. When people engage in negative thinking, it automatically triggers a state of panic or stress in the body that affects the nervous system. When the sympathetic nervous system is aroused, it results in physiological responses such as rapid heartbeat, tension in major muscle groups, and even diversion of blood circulation from major muscle groups to smaller groups, which impacts the heart, lungs, and brain. There is also the release of adrenaline and cortisol, the stress hormone, which can increase heart rate, raise blood pressure, and induce migraine headaches and other negative physiologic responses.

As the body responds physically to the initial negative thoughts, more negative thoughts are triggered by the physical response of the body over time. This continuous cycle of negative thinking triggers stress and the physiology of stress in the body, followed by more negative thoughts. More stress and its physiologic response can lead to long-term health conditions, such as cardiovascular disease, insomnia, high blood pressure, ulcers, stroke, chronic pain, migraines, a weakened immune system, and even substance abuse.

Research has found evidence that suggests negative thinking induces stress and fertility issues and slows down the body's process of healing.

Negative thinking is even more detrimental because the implications of it extend far beyond the body and brain. Negative thoughts form our attitudes, which impact our behaviors and influence our actions.

One study showed that when pessimists were faced with disappointment, they tended to develop the attitude that the situation was outside the realm of their control and made no attempt to do anything about it. Their believing the situation was outside of their control led them to disengage. Meanwhile, that same study showed that optimists tended to focus on what they can control, and as a result, they took steps to make a change.

WHAT IS POSITIVE THINKING?

Positive thinking is about adopting a mindset that approaches life's challenges with a positive outlook and a positive attitude about yourself amid flaws and mistakes. It's not the exclusion of bad events or negative characteristics about oneself but shifting to see the best in a negative situation and finding good about yourself even when flaws are present.

Psychologist Martin Seligman frames positive thinking in terms of an individual's explanatory style, or, in other words, the way you explain why events happen. Those with an optimistic explanatory style tend to give themselves credit when good things happen and blame outside forces when they experience negative outcomes. They are also more likely to see negative events as atypical and temporary.

Meanwhile, those with a pessimistic explanatory style tend to blame themselves when bad things occur and don't give themselves adequate credit when they experience success. They are also more likely to view negative events as expected and lasting.

What are the implications of positive thinking?

Positive thinking is far better for our mind, body, and behaviors. It completely counters the negative side-effects that come with negative thinking. Positive thinking increases positive emotions. Researchers have uncovered a relationship between joy and gratitude, whereby having thoughts of gratitude make us more joyful.

Positive thinking also tends to make people more resilient, being able to cope with challenges. It seems to assist people in managing stress, warding off depression, and developing vital coping tools to help them navigate challenges that arise.

The role positive thinking plays in the physical body is particularly evident in the area of immunity. A study conducted by researchers Segerstrom and Sephton found that people who were optimistic about a certain area of their lives possessed a stronger immune response than those who held a negative view of the situation.

A separate study found that activation in brain areas associated with negative thoughts and emotions led to a weaker immune response to the flu vaccine.

Additionally, positive thinking can also impact our behavior for the better. The Mayo Clinic reported several health benefits linked to optimism, including a reduced risk of death from cardiovascular problems, less depression, and a prolonged lifespan. Individuals were leading healthier lifestyles because of their optimism. Their positive attitudes and thinking helped them cope better with stress and obstacles and aided them in avoiding unhealthy behaviors. As a result, their overall health and well-being improved.

Another study demonstrated this by showing how optimists cope better with stress than pessimists. When optimists encountered a disappointment, they were more likely to focus on things they could do to solve the situation. Their positive thinking informed their behavior and led them toward a productive course of action. On the other hand, when pessimists were faced with disappointment, they simply assumed the situation was out of their control and that they were incapable of changing. In other words, their negativity formed more negativity and informed their tendency toward inaction.

OK, now that we got all that out of the way, I'm taking off the white coat, throwing down the glasses, and letting my hair down. Back to hanging out on the couch and jibber-jabbering.

So. After all that, you're saying in your head, "Great, Veronica. Now what do I do about all of this?"

First: *Learn to be a positive thinker*. There are several ways you can go about practically implementing and incorporating positive thinking in your daily life. Each of the following practices will shape your mind to think more positively so that positive attitudes can be formed, and positive actions and behaviors will follow.

Then: *Take on a COAL attitude.* COAL stands for curious, open, accepting, and loving. This is a principle promoted by a psychiatrist and mindfulness expert, Dr. Daniel Siegel, to help individuals better cope with their critical inner voice. The critical inner voice is the internal dialogue that drives our self-blame, self-loathing, and rumination. It feeds the feelings of shame and fear and leads us toward behaviors and actions that are self-limiting and self-destructive.

Adopting a COAL attitude works against the inner critic by helping us use curiosity and openness to address challenges and adversity, while simultaneously embracing ourselves with love and acceptance. Adopting this more curious and open attitude toward challenge, and a more accepting and loving attitude toward self, is a process that first begins with recognizing the negative voices and destructive thoughts you hold.

It is only through acknowledgment of those negative self-views that you can change yourself. Working to trace these negative thoughts of self back to their place of origin is the best way to completely uproot them so they can be replaced with positive thoughts. This may require working with a coach or professional to unpack situations from childhood or trauma that may have initiated the negative line of thinking about yourself you're now engaged in.

The next step in the process, after identifying negative self-views, is to practice actively stopping those thoughts when they arise in the mind. This means avoiding the tendency to allow negative thoughts to take you toward a downward spiral, halting those negative thoughts in their tracks, and consciously choosing to replace them with positive thoughts. By actively engaging and transforming negative thoughts about yourself into positive thoughts, you can transform the way you view yourself and make positive choices that align with that view.

Research from Dr. Kristin Neff indicates that self-compassion, which is generated from thinking and speaking positively about ourselves, is associated with greater emotional resilience, more caring relationship behavior, more accurate self-concepts, less reactive anger, and less narcissism.

This is because self-compassion is based on a basic sense of worth as a human being, whereas self-esteem is built upon evaluations. Thus, the self-compassion fostered via positive self-thought and self-talk allows us to relate to ourselves in a kind, connected, and clear-sighted way, even in the midst of failure, imperfection, and perceived inadequacy.

The growth mindset is the belief that your abilities can be developed. This differs from a fixed mindset, which is the belief that you are born with a certain number of fixed traits and talents. Adopting a growth mindset allows you to tap into greater inner potential and foster the same self-compassion noted in a COAL attitude.

Embodying both a growth mindset and a curious, open, accepting, and loving attitude allows you to navigate challenges with resilience and make choices that lead you toward more success, deeper understanding, and improved outcomes.

For instance, those who possess a growth mindset tend to have a more optimistic outlook that allows them to adapt better to change, better embrace challenge and risk, and have enhanced self-awareness. Each of these is necessary to transform yourself for the better.

An optimistic outlook sets the tone and expectation for how you face challenges. When you understand that a lack of present knowledge is temporary, and that the opportunity exists to gain the needed knowledge to meet and exceed the challenge, you are in a better position to thrive rather than crack under pressure.

The ability to accept change as a vital part of growth enables you to be in uncomfortable situations with a deeper understanding that discomfort and uncertainty in the present will make way for new knowledge and understanding by our process of exploration and investigation.

By embracing challenges and risk, more knowledge can be obtained and more skills can be developed. In other words, when you're uncomfortable, growth is taking place.

Affirmations are a powerful tool to change the thoughts we hold of ourselves. They reshape our inner dialogue, which for most people is critical and negative, and are a practical and intentional way to reshape the beliefs that we hold about ourselves. They can empower us to take more action in our lives. According to Dr. Walter E. Jacobson, an affirmation is a statement used to reprogram the conscious and subconscious so that we believe—and then create—the reality we desire. Affirmations help us to actualize what we want by helping us to believe, at a subconscious level, and then at a conscious level, that what we want is possible and attainable.

AFFIRMATIONS TO GET YOU STARTED

- I take care of my needs first.
- I ensure that my needs are taken care of prior to assisting others.
- I am mindful of my boundaries.
- I know where I end and others begin. I am conscious of my personal space. I respect the space of others.
- I respect my space.
- I protect my feelings and embrace my emotional security.
- I know that I need to take care of my needs before I can be there fully to take care of others.
- I honor myself, I honor others, I fill up my cup first and then give from the overflow.
- I speak my truth in a way that is kind to myself and others. I am poised under fire. I adopt personal safety practices that feel right for me while also being mindful of others.
- I am compassionate.

- I choose the highest good for myself, which becomes the highest good for others.
- I know how to balance my needs with the needs of others.
- I use kind thoughts toward myself, and I am kind to my feelings.
- The more I understand myself, the more I understand others.
- I am honest with myself, which leads to honest relationships with others.
- I see the beauty within myself, which leads to seeing the beauty in others.
- I recognize that, when I create balance within myself, it is reflected in my relationships with others.
- When I take care of myself first, I have the energy and resources to take care of others.

REFLECTION QUESTIONS

1. Why is putting my oxygen mask on first vitally important?
2. How does setting boundaries with others help me?
3. Where can I practice new boundaries at home, work, and with friends?

6

SURRENDER TO YOUR SPIRIT

One thing I often hear from people is that they want to be their true selves. They're walking around with the feeling of not being true, and it feels like impostor syndrome.

How do you figure out who you are and how you're supposed to show up in the world? There are several ways to do that. You might know about popular tools like astrology and natal charts, Kolbe assessments, and enneagrams. There are also ways to figure out who you are that are based on your anatomy.

In this section, I will discuss the three parts of the spiritual You. First is your spiritual DNA, second is how to cultivate your spiritual fruits, and third is how to develop your spiritual intelligence.

This is an area that is fun to explore, one that you can fall into easily with an open mind and spirit, if you're pointed in the right direction.

You are going to get there, but if you choose to stay stuck, it will be the long and hard way. Sometimes, staying stuck is simply part of your spiritual journey and where you need to be. What works best, to move forward toward a life in which you receive respect and appreciation, is to stop following other people's plans and start following your own. Get out of the habit of imitating somebody else's life. Create your own.

When I look at spiritual matters—how we come to understand our spiritual path and decide which road is the right road—I see that few parents were taught what spirituality means. How are parents expected to teach their children to honor their spirit when they've never been taught how to honor their own spirits? This area can spur heated discussions.

There are those who follow a religious path with its accompanying stringent doctrine. This doctrine may or may not be working for them, but it's what they know, so they keep following it. Generally, we come to a particular religious doctrine because that's how we were brought up. It's about who our parents allowed themselves to be around us. To keep fitting in, you embraced what you were taught. This silent nod allows you to remain part of the family and community.

In so many instances, making the decision to walk away from the religious tribe bestowed on you at birth can lead to abandonment by family and friends. Therefore, we are reluctant to walk away from religious teachings because we have that fear of being alone, of not being accepted, and of abandonment. We all want unconditional love and acceptance. We all want to be part of the crowd. Religion is one of those areas where, if you walk like them, talk like them, act like them, and believe like them, you're rewarded with belonging.

But what about the spirit? What is this spirit and where does it fit in? How do we figure out how to honor our spirit and how to be who we are?

Since you chose to read this book, I'm certain you've asked this question a lot. You've realized that you may think differently, act differently, and believe differently from those you love and from what you've been taught. How do you reconcile this? One way is to realize that everyone is on a diffcrent spiritual journey. You were placed in the presence of your family. It is you that chose to be with them in the life between lives. Your soul decided that there was something to be learned from being a part of that family, or that group of friends, going to that school, and living in that community. And here you are reading this book. Your spirit and soul journey have led you to this book.

To move your spirit in a direction that is right for you, let's go through the three areas that will develop and evolve your spirit in a way that is unique and authentic to you. These teachings will also allow you to understand and accept the spiritual journey of others in your sphere more easily. By having a framework to understand your spiritual journey, you accept other people with different spiritual journeys, even those who love you and care for you, and who don't have completely different spiritual journeys. You will make different choices for yourself, which will make your life go in a different way. This is where my spiritual journey has led me in these three areas.

First, the oldest area in my spiritual journey is being born into a family who subscribed to Christianity. One New Testament verse I have had in my head is from the book of Galatians.

"But the fruit of the Spirit is love, joy, peace, patience, kindness, goodness, faithfulness, gentleness, self-control; against such things there is no law."
— *Galatians 5:22 to 23, English Standard Version*

(I want to assure you this isn't going to be a Bible study. In fact, it's going to be something quite different, you'll soon see.)

Anyone of any faith, or no faith at all, can use this concept of fruits of the Spirit. The fruits of the Spirit are emotions that can inform your actions.

Even though you may have lost a particular religious path, or you have decided that a religious path is not serving you, there are going to be lessons in that religious path that, in your journey, helped to develop your spirit in a way that evolved you to a different level. Be grateful and joyful for the religious path you have traveled, that has led you to some pains and some realizations about what works for you and what does not, on a spiritual level. You are here right now to read this and draw upon that path, to understand how your growth in the spiritual was, as opposed to the religious unit.

In this step of The R.E.S.P.E.C.T. Method, we're putting aside the religion and going for the spiritual only. That doesn't mean you have to shun your religion. It's not either/or. It's both, because the only right way to travel on your journey is to have it unfold step by step in little pieces, and only you know which steps to choose. No one else can decide for you which steps to take.

If you have a religious practice that serves you well, which, at least 51 percent of the time, brings you gratitude, love, and joy, then keep it, and be open to adding other practices that will make it even better.

However, if you're on a religious path that causes you fear, anger, or sadness, or that makes you feel that you are motivated by fear, anger, or sadness from those religious teachings, it may be time for you to evaluate whether to move on or away. Go back to Chapter 5, Evaluate Your Thinking.

Perhaps there's a different way for you to think about it, or perhaps that religion really isn't serving you anymore. If you do decide to walk in a different direction from a religion, be confident that there's still a loving universe out there that will embrace and help you.

SPIRITUAL ATTRACTION

When I first wrote this chapter, I didn't want to go too deeply into these spiritual matters, especially regarding the system of Human Design. I didn't want you to get bogged down in the details. But there are some details that explain those invisible phenomena that are happening when we interact with people. That includes family, friends, coworkers, and most importantly, romantic partners, but all are equally important.

What's going on here? Why do some people just rub us the wrong way and other people it's just like animal magnetism?

I want to explain a little bit about what attracts us and repels us from certain people. I haven't seen a lot of explanation in the traditional/conventional scientific literature about this. This is all spiritual—it's how we feel when we're interacting with someone else.

We meet someone and we feel either (a) they're a good energy and we like being around them or (b) they're not good energy and we just don't have any feeling that we want to even be near them. That can happen with people you work with, bosses, and family members.

This can happen especially with potential romantic partners, too. When you focus on superficial qualities, they seem perfectly fine on paper, but there's just something that's not clicking. With other people, you may not be able to pinpoint exactly what about them makes you want to be around them, but you know there's some connection there.

This is the point where, if you haven't thought about getting your Human Design done, this is where you want to do it. Go to drveronica.com/human-design-bodygraph-request because you're going to want to have yours in front of you when you're processing what I'm going to teach you in the following section.

I'll start off with a story. I was talking to my favorite cousin Elena recently. When she first went off to college, I was already in college, too, so I was a bit older. We hadn't been in contact, but what I did know is she came back from her year at college with a baby. Many years later, in our adulthood, we had a chance to discuss what happened at that time of life, to get past all the emotion.

Now, with her adult child, she said, "I remember I went someplace, and I saw his father, and suddenly it was like—I don't know if I believe this anymore—love at first sight. I saw him, and it was like immediately I had to be with him. He and I got to know each other, started dating, and voilà, we ended up with a son together."

What happened? Is there such a thing as love at first sight?

Let me tell you what could be happening. Look at the Human Design chart. There are spiritual mechanics of attraction. There are these things called hanging gates, open centers, imprinting, genetics, and unmet spiritual energy needs.

When you look on the chart and you see all these lines, and a lot of the lines just seem to stop in mid-air, that means you're going to be attracted to somebody who has the other half of the line that's also stopping in mid-air. That's your unmet need. We're all looking for our other half.

We also have what are called centers, and in Human Design, there are nine. When they're colored in, they're considered defined, meaning you have the energy that's already there. And when they're open, they're called undefined.

When we have undefined centers, we're looking for somebody with a defined center. We're looking for somebody with that particular energy. For somebody like Elena who has an undefined sacral center, she's going to be attracted to somebody who has a defined sacral center. We're looking to fill our unmet energetic needs.

Another component of spiritual attraction is imprinting. Imprinting is a phenomenon that comes from our family of origin. We grow up with them, and we take on (or imprint) their spiritual and energetic patterns. When it's not really us but it's a pattern that we find in our family of origin from being around this, we take on other people's energies.

You might find that, in other types of relationships besides romantic relationships and family relationships, you can take on other people's energy. You might realize you have a good friend, and the two of you go so well together, it just always feels great to be with them. After being with them for a long time, you become more alike, because your energy systems are taking on each other's energy systems.

This is all the invisible woo-woo stuff that nobody talks about generally, but this is what happens, so I encourage you to look at what's going on here in some of these areas.

WHAT ELSE CREATES ATTRACTION?

We have those electromagnetic hanging gates, the lines in the chart that are pulling toward other people who have the other half of the line. We also have patterns of conditioning, your centers being open, imprinting, generational energy patterns, and genetics.

But the other piece that's fascinating is the unmet energetic need. People say unmet needs is the same as being needy, but we all are needy in our energetic patterns. This is what often makes relationships hard to break up. A specific pattern makes certain people feel out of sorts when their relationships are broken up.

One center is called the splenic center, and if yours is open when you're with someone who has a defined center and then you break apart, you can feel really needy, like something was torn away from you.

These spiritual phenomena that show up in places like our Human Design can explain a lot about this magnetism that we have for certain people.

One thing to understand here is that magnetism does not equal real love. Magnetism does not necessarily equal your soul mate because real love is built from what people do in their relationship over time. You can have perfectly synced spiritual designs that go together and have a relationship still not work because it's not the only thing that makes a relationship work or not work.

But when you put two charts together, when you put two people together with two different spiritual designs, it may explain what makes certain relationships work and others not work. Again, this includes romantic partners, as well as family, friends, and bosses. For some people, it works together well. For other people, they're just repulsive to each other. You can see two ends of the spectrum. There are certain energies you're going to love and certain energies you're not going to love.

Your Human Design

To get the most out of this section, get your Human Design done by me personally for free, if you haven't done so already. Your report comes with free videos to provide you with a more detailed explanation than I can give in this book because it's so very important for you to know who you are from a spiritual perspective. Just go to: drveronica.com/human-design-bodygraph-request

Human Design is a way to find out who you are, what your spiritual DNA looks like, and who the authentic spiritual You is. It is something that you are born with. For instance, if you're a person like me, who falls outside of the 70 percent of generator types in which most other people are categorized, you might feel a little bit weird.

The Human Design system was originated in 1987 by Alan Robert Krakower, later known as Ra Uru Hu. This brilliant system is a way to see, feel, and understand your unique spiritual blueprint. Human Design describes your spiritual genes. Your design is unique to you, in the same way that your genes are unique to you. When I coach my clients, I always ask on their intake application—before I even meet them—for their birth information, telling them that I use Human Design to work in coaching my clients.

I have to thank one of my fellow authors who also coached me in this area. Robin Winn, author of *Understanding Your Clients Through Human Design*, masterfully guided me to better use my own type in the Human Design system as a projector. In addition to having more ease in my romantic partnership with my husband, and using the right strategies in running my business, I have incorporated the Human Design system to help my clients understand themselves in a different way. This understanding has allowed me to guide them to get what they want in their health, finances, relationships, and career, in addition to spirituality.

Human Design is a combination of astrology, the I Ching, Kabbalah, and the chakra system, which was a system that was given to a gentleman in 1987. As you can see, it puts together several well-known energetic systems. However, those other systems don't correspond one-to-one with the Human Design system. It is its own unique and separate system.

I'm going to briefly go over the five Human Design types here, but I also invite you to have your chart done. I will do it and send it to you, with an audio and a video in which you can learn a little bit more about your type, along with some other key elements of Human Design to get you started in understanding.

Even though I will go into a brief description about each type, it may not mean a lot to you at this point, especially until you know your type, but bear with me. This is important because it involves the energies of our auras that interact with everyone else's energies and auras. You might notice at times that you are in great synchronicity with somebody else when you're with them, and at other times, you aren't. It could be because your designs and your strategies are quite different. Once you understand your design and other peoples' designs, it will allow you to find compassion for yourself and compassion for others.

In the Human Design system, there are five types that determine a main strategy for life. The five types are:

1. Generator
2. Manifesting generator
3. Projector
4. Manifestor
5. Reflector

Generators cover about 35 percent of the population, and another 35 percent are manifesting generators. That means 70 percent of people are generators of some kind. That leaves 30 percent for the projectors, manifestors, and reflectors.

Following the strategy of your Human Design in everyday life is quite important, but it's a major challenge when you have no one to help you sit back, understand yourself, and develop the necessary patience to have life go your way. For example, if you're a projector and you use the same strategy as someone who is not a projector, then you will feel completely out of sorts, and wonder why the opportunities that seem to work and present themselves to other people won't seem to work well for you. You'll be working harder because you're working against the flow of your spirit and your design, or your spiritual DNA.

Here's a little bit about all the different designs. It's much easier in life to get what you want when you go with your own flow. Knowing about yourself through the Human Design system illustrates to you what that flow is. Let's go over what the different types are, some of their key traits, and the strategies that work and don't work to get what they want from jobs and relationships.

Generators

The beauty of the generator is that they are full of energy, vitality, and purpose. Knowing what their unique work is (and doing it) is the key to their happiness and living into their spiritual destination or spiritual destiny.

Generators are the workforce of humanity. Before you say, "Oh my gosh, I'm just one of the workforces of humanity," I want you to know there are some famous generators, such as Oprah and the Dalai Lama. You fall into the same category of people with some great shoes to fill.

Generators have sustainable energy, which means they can go and go, and they may not need a whole lot of sleep. They seem to be able to just keep going when everybody else might not be able to.

They have an inner guidance system that seemingly allows them to know just what to do. That inner guidance system is driven by yes/no questions, not open-ended questions. If you are communicating with someone who is a generator, you want to ask them yes/no questions. It's easy for them to answer that, but when you ask them an open-ended question, they seem to be flummoxed and flabbergasted.

Let me remind you that a full 70 percent of the population are generators or manifesting generators, so assume that someone is a generator until you know. If someone is not a generator, then you'll know it because they'll give more explanation after their yes/no answers. Generators answer yes or no with no follow-up explanation and are quite happy with that.

Generators thrive when they find their work, and they master it. If you discover that you are a generator, and you have burned out, you're probably asking yourself, "What happened to me and my sustainable energy? I don't have sustainable energy. What's going on?" This happens when you go against your nature and say yes to things that should be a no, or when you're working in an area that is not your area of mastery.

If you're reading this book because you burned out, and you're looking for a different way to operate, then you must go back and figure out where you started saying yes when the answer should have been a no. A yes can become a no, and a no can become a yes, so as a generator, you must continuously check in with your inner guidance system.

Trust deeply in your inner guidance, even in situations like jobs or relationships. It can lead you in a different direction, which might have been wrong before but is right now and vice versa. If you're doing a certain kind of work and you have felt good about it and it was a big yes, there might be a time where that work becomes a no and you burn out. If you're at a job or in a career where you're starting to feel bad about it, maybe it's already become a no, and it's time to find and master another area of work.

Generators are good in relationships. They're relational. Notice how you work in relation to other people. Most of the time, you are good on a team and in a relationship. But, if you're on a team or in a relationship that's not working for you, then perhaps it has become a no, or maybe you're in a relationship with someone who doesn't need relationships the way you do, because they have a different design.

Manifesting generator

The difference between a generator and manifesting generator is the ability to initiate action. Manifesting generators are initiators and workers at the same time. They have the vocal capacity and therefore have this power. To the rest of us, these people look superhuman. The manifesting generator seems able to easily get situations to go their way while the rest of the world listens to and follows them.

Gandhi, Mother Teresa, and Martin Luther King Jr. are famous manifesting generators. Donald Trump and Hillary Clinton are also both manifesting generators. (Don't get in a bad mood politically now. This is about understanding spiritual DNA and Human Design. What great examples these two individuals are of the manifesting generator energy.)

How are all these people the same spiritual type? It depends on how you use your spiritual DNA that makes it come off. Notice that all these people are charismatic only to a certain type of person they attract—not necessarily to everybody.

The gifts of the manifesting generator are that they can be heard and make things happen. They're able to impact people and situations. They empower people, but they have the capacity to act on their own as well, without other people helping them. They can easily act independently, and they do not thrive on relationships. They're able to multitask, and they can be prolific.

If this sounds like you, then you are a manifesting generator. It means that you can initiate, and you can be seen and heard and have great impact on people. You can keep going because you also have the inner GPS of a manifestor.

The challenge of being a manifesting generator is that, when people don't necessarily know what you're going to do, they can be caught off-guard. You have to learn to tell people what you're going to do. You tend to be an individualistic, loner-type of person who does things on your own without the need for other people or relationships.

Manifesting generators can come off as frustrated and angry. And sometimes they lack focus and skip steps or burn out.

If you're a manifesting generator, your upside is that you're able to work indefinitely, and you can initiate and create from your ideas and put them into action. The downside is that, when you're not informing and communicating your intent with family, friends, and work colleagues, it can lead to frustration and anger in other people and, ultimately, within you.

Projectors

Projectors are about 20 percent of the population. Yours truly is a projector, and I have several clients who are projectors, so I will dive a bit deeper here.

If you're a projector, you feel out of sorts because you are around generators most of the time, which can pull you into feeling like you must be like them and be on the go all the time. You can't figure out why you can't work like them. You're not having the impact they are. But you can have big impact in the world guiding people. You're like the diamond in the rough. You must understand that your life will differ greatly from your average generator.

If you have burned out early in your career, it is worth looking to see if you are a projector. Projectors do not have sustainable, unending energy like generators do. Therefore, as a projector, you must protect your energy because you're prone to burnout. Why? Because your destiny in life is to be a wise guide rather than a worker.

Now, everyone says they want to be a guide, but it can be hard to be the guide.

Once you embrace the spiritual You as a projector, your first order of business is to learn how to *be* and to stop doing so much. You must be selective and discriminating about what you choose to take on. You must continuously refocus on what you are going to *be*, which is what will make you the most valuable, for yourself and in the world. You must strip back everything and *be*—and wait to be invited. The opportunities will come to you. Trust that they will, but only if you *be*. How is this? Because of your unique aura.

The auric energy of the projector is magnetic, but remember, a magnet has two sides. And if you turn it around, a magnet can repel. With the magnetic aura, the right people, opportunities, and situations will come toward you when you wait. They will be in your universe, in your aura. When you wait, the part of you that attracts will continue to attract. The worst thing you can do as a projector is chase because that's like turning around your magnet and repelling with it.

Your strategy for life is to wait for the invitation and wait for recognition, which means you can't just go after everything. You must wait for somebody to recognize that you're there and ask specifically for your help.

Interestingly, this goes against what everyone is usually told, to be go-getters, to go after what they want. As a projector, if you decide to pursue someone or something, you will repel people and opportunities. It therefore makes you invisible—not seen or heard.

I can tell you how crappy it feels to do lots of work and be left out of the recognition. In fact, I have been on prominent committees, and when the members were acknowledged publicly, I have been left out of articles and websites.

The fact is you don't need to pursue recognition because you have an aura that attracts people to you for your natural ability to guide. Projectors have a unique quality of *being*. This means that, without doing anything, people simply enjoy the aura and energy of projectors, who are pleasant to be around even when they are not saying or doing anything. Projectors are known as people with "good energy."

As a projector, remember to project away from yourself onto other people because you're best recognized and invited when you focus on other people and away from yourself. Shine the light on others as much as possible.

You can do this with the language you use. Manifestors and manifesting generators tend to frame context with the "I," as in, "here's what I'm going to teach you" or "here's who I am." Projectors will do well to frame context with "you" (and sometimes with "we"), as in, "here's what you will learn" or "here's how we can work together."

This may seem somewhat counterintuitive because this is not how we're taught.

If you're in a normal conversation and you have something to offer, wait for somebody to ask for your opinion. It may be a long, long time before someone asks, but when they do finally ask, things can blossom for you.

One of the best ways to get opportunities as a projector is to have someone else introduce you. A lot of the big opportunities that have come to me have been through other people introducing me to someone else. Or they have found me through a big stage or another opportunity. People find me when I speak, or they meet me and find something interesting on my website, or they ask a question. I'll say, "Here's what I know. By the way, here's how I know this." Because they've asked me for my opinions, my coaching is welcome.

Let's back up a moment to show how this plays out in relationships. Some of you are leaning forward right now because you're a projector in a relationship with a non-projector.

Waiting is key, even in relationships. How I show up as a projector wife is important. A projector with a manifesting generator, for example, makes for a good couple.

When I want to offer my opinion about some topic to my husband, I ask him first. "Would you like to know what I'm thinking about this?" I've worded it in a yes/no manner because he is a manifesting generator, and the generator part wins out in questioning, so a yes/no question is best.

But I've also asked, and you might say this sounds childish. Why should you have to ask as an adult? My projector design is repelling unless I am invited, so the way I get myself invited is to ask him if he wants to know my opinion. See how I am honoring both my design and his design?

If I go ahead and just give him my opinion, I can tell you it's going to cause him irritation, a fight might come, and I won't even know where it came from, other than from going against this invisible thing inside our Human Designs.

Before I knew about Human Design, I didn't understand a lot of what was going on in our relationship. My husband's reaction to me when I offered help was bizarre in my eyes. But, after incorporating my projector strategy and honoring his manifesting generator design, there is now more ease—until I fall back into throwing my opinion around without being invited.

If I ask him, "Would you like to know my opinion?" and he says, "no," I zip my lips. I wait for another time. Usually, very soon after he says "no," he will come back and ask for my opinion, because I've honored his answer, I've honored my design, and I've honored his design. Learning how to be a patient projector in romantic relationships, with family and friends, and in professional circumstances, allows life to go smoother. Wait for recognition and the invitation. That can be incredibly challenging, especially when you're not used to doing it.

As a projector, you can move things toward getting invited. Place yourself in multiple situations so that you will be in the right place at the right time to get the invitation. This is worth mentioning again: one highly effective way to get an invitation is through an introduction. I work a lot with my projector clients on how to be patient and wait for their invitations. I then help them to realize and examine times in their lives when they didn't wait for the invitation. Things didn't go so well. But when they did wait for the invitation, opportunities opened beautifully. When you fall into your spiritual design as a projector, the right people and the right situations will come. And you will know exactly when to say yes and when to say no, too.

One thing about being the wise guide is that there are going to be people who "get you" super well when you have a freak genius channel. And there are going to be other people who are the exact opposite. They just think you are hog wild bat-crap crazy. You might have noticed that sometimes things go so well, and other times they fall so flat and low. Even when you've been invited and you have the freak genius channel, that can happen.

Manifestors

Eight percent to 9 percent of the population are manifestors. Manifestors are people who can initiate action. And it seems like the world just follows. They can have amazing impact on people and, with that strong throat, speaking and being heard is one of their magical gifts. They're natural leaders, and independent. Some famous manifestors: Frida Kahlo, Maya Angelou, Adolf Hitler, George W. Bush, Mao Zedong, Martha Stewart, Jesse Jackson, and Susan Sarandon.

When you're a manifestor, you have an initiator power hand, but also you have a repelling aura. A repelling aura doesn't mean you are repulsive or that people don't like you. It does seem that sometimes you are extraordinary at intimidating people. It's that personal quality of independence, which can sometimes be off-putting to people.

One of the ways to help people understand you is to inform before you act. You can act and initiate and have great success. However, if you want to be understood, especially in your relationships, make sure you have informed before you act, so that people don't become resentful. Informing before you act can counteract the rippling of your aura and help people accept you more easily. But know that you have the immense ability, the natural ability, to be a leader. You are a natural leader; you don't even have to do anything. You are like the Pied Piper, you go out there, you say something, and all of a sudden, you have a lot of people who follow you along immediately and instantaneously. And that's the beauty of being a manifestor.

My friend Sarah Jane is a manifestor. When Sarah Jane sends a text and says, "Hey people, do you want to do this?" All of a sudden, the answers come in with "Yes, yes, yes, yes." She initiated what she asked, and people followed her lead. It's amazing to watch. Contrast that with a projector who sends out a text to forty people, and says, "Hey, do you want to join my mastermind group?" They will hear only crickets because they invited others rather than waited to be invited. See how much difference this spiritual design makes?

Reflectors

The reflectors are 1 percent to 2 percent of the population. They are the clear mirror seemingly without their own self because they mirror whomever they encounter. The reflector is like a chameleon in that they can blend in practically anywhere. This is an interesting state of being because as a reflector, a lot of times, you can't figure out who you are and where you end and someone else begins. This can be quite exhausting and confusing.

Because reflectors are absorbing all the energy around them, it can exhaust their own energy. Reflectors don't have the motor energy center defined that keeps them going. Therefore, they need a lot of alone time to rejuvenate themselves. Reflectors are one with nature. A lot of times, reflectors feel more in touch with the animals, trees, and plants than they do with other humans. Reflectors are the most bright and awakened beings.

Reflectors can seem to just disappear or become invisible in a room. Their energy is such that they may not be noticed at all.

The Freak/Genius Channel

Of all the clients I've worked with, a lot of people tend to be attracted to others who have similar Human Designs. You might have this piece in your design, and that could be a blessing.

There is a channel called the freak/genius channel (the 43-23 channel). The freak/genius channel is one of those things where people see you, when you open your mouth, as either an absolute genius or a crazy freak. That freak/genius channel in a projector, for instance, is fascinating and is particular to projectors, although you don't have to be a projector to have this channel.

Human Design Examples of My Clients

One of my coaches once asked me how I get clients. I answered, "They just seem to fall out of the sky." Remember that if you're a projector. People must be around you, in your aura, to learn who you are, and to be able to see and experience how wise you are.

While they're learning more about you, you may not even know that they're around. Many of the clients who find me may be in my universe for years before they decide that it's time to work with me. I don't even know that they are there or are aware of me. On the other hand, people may find me and decide right away that they want to work with me because they're so attracted to the aura.

Both Dr. Sydney and Anna are projectors. Dr. Sydney and Anna understood before they met me that something was different about them. Dr. Sydney, prior to meeting me, had heard about Human Design, and she said it was on her radar. But she hadn't quite comprehended what she was intuitive enough to understand. Dr. Sydney's daughter is a manifestor and understands at her young age how to be an initiator and leader. Dr. Sydney felt that it was almost magical for her daughter that she could make things happen as a manifestor, even as a preschool-aged person.

On the other hand, she couldn't quite understand, as a projector, how to make things happen in her life. It was just arduous, always pushing uphill. It was easy for her to be misunderstood or completely ignored. At times, there was also the matter of the sheer exhaustion and burnout she experienced even before reaching midcareer. The physical, mental, and emotional exhaustion made it hard for her to do her demanding sixty- to eighty-hours-a-week job as a physician at times, and to show up in life. She kept pushing along, but this was affecting her physical health, causing her to gain weight that she couldn't figure out how to lose.

As a projector, Anna also realized that a lot of times, on her job and in her relationships, both romantic and with family and friends, she knew how to solve problems. Yet, it seemed that when she had the right answer, she wasn't acknowledged or appreciated. It was almost like she was invisible because others, including her ex-partner, saw the brilliant ideas that she offered as their own rather than her genius. She wasn't being seen, as she wasn't being heard. She was not appreciated, which is why her ex-partner walked out on her.

To add some more interest, when looking at her ex-partner's Human Design, I noted that he had the "searching" channel, which means that he would always be looking for the next thing and a different way of seeing something. He was always in pursuit of something else, even when he didn't know it. It was in his spiritual design to be in pursuit.

For projectors, it can be challenging to be seen and heard for their wants, needs, and desires, because their spiritual design has an energy that necessitates waiting to be recognized and invited to participate. Anna's ex wasn't seeing and hearing her wants, needs, and desires, and he was living his own spiritual design of pursuit.

Learning to wait for the invitation was exceedingly difficult for Anna because she felt the right answer was to pursue her ex-partner. Yet for the projector, pursuit is like the kiss of death. The aura of the projector is attractive when they wait and repels when they pursue. Therefore, the more Anna chased, the faster her partner (and any partner) would move away.

One day, coincidentally ending up on the same train ride with her ex-boyfriend, Anna decided to pull it back a little, rather than bombard him to talk about fixing their broken relationship. She had passed him on the train as she was going to the train's café car ahead. His head was down reading when she passed. In this instance, coming back, she decided to test out the projector strategy of waiting for recognition and an invitation. So, she just walked by, said hello calmly, and kept moving, counter to what she wanted to do, which was to aggressively pursue a conversation. She decided to wait to see how the situation was going to unfold. When she walked by and said hello and kept going, he looked up, stopped her, and said, "Anna, good to see you. Why don't you come sit with me and we can chat a little bit?" This was a marked difference from all the times where she had been texting him, emailing him, and calling him, and he had not answered her. She previously wondered, "Why does he keep ignoring me? He at least owes me an answer when I text him, or email him, or call him."

The important piece about this is to understand the spiritual energy as a projector in this situation. The aura is repelling when they chase a situation or person. But when projectors wait calmly and patiently, their auras are naturally attractive to other people. It brings in other people. We're taught in life to go after what we want—and that includes a partner. Anna desperately wanted her partner back, so her strategy was to do everything possible, which meant to call, to email, or to text, and chase. Whereas what works is to honor her projector spirit and realize how wonderful things can evolve. Patience serves the projector.

Another client of mine, Dr. Maggie, is a generator. She started her coaching program with me feeling listless in her career and was uncertain of which direction she should be going in next. Generators are meant to go, go, go, and they are happy when they find the work they love, when they're doing exactly the work they are meant to do. I pointed out to Maggie what happens when generators say yes to something that should be a no. When generators say yes and stay in a situation they should not be in, whether it be work or relationship, that's when burnout occurs. If you are a generator and you have succumbed to burnout, you need to step back and figure out what it is that you're saying yes to that you should be saying no. To get over your burnout, you must summon up the courage to get out of that job or relationship because you're not going to be able to rejuvenate until you do that. Generators can go indefinitely, but only when they are in their yes situations.

Your Spiritual Fruit

Now that you understand a bit about your Human Design and have gotten some guidance about how to live into it, the next component in surrendering your spirit is to cultivate your spiritual fruits. This is a concept that anyone who has read the Bible will understand—the spiritual fruits are of love, joy, peace, patience, kindness, goodness, faithfulness, gentleness, and self-control.

I want you to think about cultivating the fruits of your spirit, in these different ways, toward you. In a lot of religions, we're taught to cultivate these fruits toward the world. However, before you can give anything to the world, you have to cultivate them within yourself. I want you to think of this first when you think about the fruit of the Spirit. I recommend you cultivate, every week, one of these fruits of the Spirit toward yourself.

Love

What can you do to love yourself? Pick one task that will love yourself, a task that you can do every single day to demonstrate love to yourself.

Joy

What brings you joy? Write it down every day. Pick something that brings you joy. Before anyone else, you deserve joy.

Peace

What gives you peace? What can you do that will calm your mind so that you feel peaceful and can sustain that feeling? Is there something that you need to eliminate from your life to give you peace? Is there something you must add to your life to give you peace?

Patience

How can you have patience with yourself? When did you become impatient toward yourself? Do you realize that if you have patience toward yourself, sometimes everything happens much quicker by being patient? The universe, God, the creator of all, that is what shows up when you're quiet enough to notice. When you have patience with yourself, you'll start noticing all the miracles that happen in your life. And patience has a way of accelerating and manifesting all kinds of things, no matter what your spiritual type is.

Kindness

How can you be kind to yourself? What can you do to be kinder to yourself? Maybe it's time to stop running those marathons. Maybe it's time to sleep late. Maybe it's time to get a babysitter so you can just be alone. How can you be kinder to yourself? Perhaps you could be kind by taking four weeks of vacation.

Goodness

What's good for you? What's right for you? How do you show up in the world? What is good for you and good for everyone else around you? Goodness requires wisdom and knowledge of you to show up as the real you. When you show up as the real you, goodness easily follows.

Faithfulness

Do you have faith in you? Have you lost faith in you? How do you get back the faith in you? One of the ways you can get back into faith in yourself is to examine these five areas of your life: health, money, career and purpose, relationships, and spirituality and personal growth. When can you regain your faith in each of these areas for yourself? This is all about habits. Perhaps you've developed some habits that have made you lose faith in yourself. How do you regain that faith? By looking at one habit in each area, and making one little change in each area. Develop one habit every twenty-one days to read and develop faith in yourself. Faithfulness is a habit. Once you practice faithfulness, you will have it down. There's a way to develop the muscle of faithfulness in you.

Gentleness

Many people are so hard on themselves. Do you have that critical inner voice going on? Be gentle with yourself. Practice self-compassion. Compassion starts with treating You gently. Self-control is wrapped up with patience and gentleness.

Self-Control

Learn to take deep breaths. One of the best ways to have self-control is through deep breathing. Self-control happens when you get out of the fight-or-flight reaction and get into the rest-and-digest reaction. Self-control happens in the parasympathetic state, not the sympathetic state. How do you develop self-control? You develop self-control by counting to ten before you say or do anything, especially when you want to react. Simple yet challenging, right? Here's a special way to count to ten. Deep breath in, deep breath out, count to four for each breath. Breathe in—one, two, three, four. Breathe out—one, two, three, four. That's one cycle. When you do that ten times, you'll have self-control. Cultivate the fruits of your spirit toward you.

YOUR SPIRITUAL QUOTIENT

The third piece of surrendering to your spirit is raising your SQ, your spiritual quotient. This has been laid out well by Danah Zohar and Ian Marshall. According to their book, *Spiritual Capital*, there are twelve areas of spiritual intelligence. The next step for those developing their spirit, no matter what your type is, is to think about the areas of spiritual intelligence that you display outwardly. The fruits of the Spirit display inward spiritual intelligence, while you develop and display outward spiritual intelligence.

The 12 areas of spiritual intelligence

1. Self-awareness. Knowing what you believe in.
2. Spontaneity. Living in the moment of now and being responsive today, not tied to the past or the future.
3. Acting from your deep beliefs and values and living accordingly. This is walking the walk and talking the talk—congruently, in harmony.

4. Understanding your connectivity to everything and everybody. Knowing that it all matters.
5. Compassion. Showing concern for others and developing universal sympathy. You're able to put yourself in a lot of different shoes and understand others in a deep, meaningful way.
6. Celebration of diversity. Valuing different people and different situations.
7. Independence. Being able to stand against the crowd.
8. Asking "why" or being eternally curious. This refers to the need to understand things and get to the bottom of them.
9. The ability to reframe. Being able to stand back, look at a situation, and put it in a different manner, the ability to see it in a different way.
10. Positive use of adversity. Rolling with the punches and making beauty from ashes.
11. Humility. Being able to look at yourself introspectively, see what's going on, and understand that you're a player in a larger world.
12. A sense of vocation. Knowing what you can do and your purpose.

RECAP

There are three areas to consider in surrendering to your spirit:

First, learn your spiritual DNA and understand it. Just like your physical DNA, you're born with spiritual DNA. This is done through the Human Design system. Learn to work with it because it's wonderful, it's beautiful, and it's who you are.

Second, cultivate your spiritual fruits. This involves taking action toward yourself in the areas of love, joy, peace, patience, kindness, goodness, faithfulness, gentleness, and self-control.

Third, raise your spiritual quotient. In other words, become spiritually intelligent by exploring and developing in the twelve areas that will facilitate the process to outwardly display these concepts.

To work through the fruits of the Spirit, consciously practice one of these attributes each week. To work through the spiritual quotient, work on one per month. You can easily map out your entire year to remind yourself what the theme of each month is, and what the theme of each week is. Self-awareness is happiness as you consciously evaluate and create small but implementable tasks you can do in each of these areas. As you use your spiritual muscles regularly, you will know yourself better and have more clarity about how you can show up in all kinds of situations based on your spiritual design and your spiritual values.

This chapter is long because it's rare that we're taught how to develop our spirit, especially outside of religion. This is all about figuring out who you are, the unique and authentic *you* that we all yearn to be. Part of it is in your design. How do you use it? You cultivate the fruits of the Spirit within yourself, and you master spiritual intelligence by working on your spiritual quotient.

7

PAUSE

You need this long discussion and definition of the pause. Stop doing stuff. Sit down. Take a break. Do nothing. I hear you saying, "I know what a pause is," or, "I know, I need to take a break." There's a buzzy trend going on right now with all these people confessing they need more self-care. It's empty talk by most women, though. Too-busy women say to themselves frequently, "I need to do more self-care."

But how many of you are committed to do the type of self-care that mirrors the care and attention you give to others in your life? Very few of you.

Don't be embarrassed or ashamed. Once you finish this step of The R.E.S.P.E.C.T. Method, you'll have made progress toward getting there. No transformation can happen without the time and space for it to happen, so even though this is smack in the middle of the method, taking a pause is best done first before any of the other steps. However, stopping and taking a break from work, family, and other commitments alone is such a scary and threatening concept to so many of you, I buried it in the middle.

For several years now, I've been in a coaching program called

Strategic Coach, run by Dan Sullivan, who is known as the man who has trained many great entrepreneurs, including Peter Diamandis, Joe Polish, and Dean Jackson. Dan created the concept of the Entrepreneurial Time System, which I share with all my clients.

He teaches that the goal is to have as many free days as possible. To be creative and keep going, you need as much free time as you can take. What qualifies as free time, a free day, is a complete twenty-four hours from midnight to midnight. With nothing related to work or even errands, it's just time for you to do anything that you want to do. That's rejuvenation. If you want to walk around, if you want to watch TV, if you want to read fiction—that's what your free day can be spent doing. Going to the spa, going for a hike. That's free time. What's not free time is vacation with your family, which is something you have to plan, organize, and have stress from.

A free day is twenty-four hours of not reading email, not answering texts, nothing but pleasure activities, in order to have time to rejuvenate and empty out your brain. The concept of the pause is based on this free time, where you're only going to do activities that relate to you.

Nothing else, not work, not spouses, and not children. You cannot read business email. You can't read business books. You can only participate in activities that are meant to allow your spirit and your brain to relax. For more to come into your life, you must have space for more to come into your life.

Let's talk about how this plays out in a relationship. You're not going to bring the best you can possibly bring to any type of relationship, whether it be romantic or family and friends, unless you have the time to put into that relationship. The time to go on dates, and to spend time with that person, getting to know them in the relationship, is necessary to have the situation evolve to more permanency. You need time to be attentive to what's going on with you first, and then what's going on with the other person, allowing mutual respect and deep love to form. You must have time.

Next, you need the energy. You have to be clear and strong to show up as the best you. It is time to admit that when you're tired, you're irritable, angry, and you're the big B word. You fall apart mentally when life doesn't go perfectly because you don't have the mental capacity to be patient and think about the best way to handle a situation to your benefit. You get to the point where you don't even have the physical capacity to go through everyday life.

How does this play in the work situation? Well, a lot of people decide that it's a good idea to work long days and long hours, including nights and weekends. In addition, although they may have vacation allotted by their job, they don't take it. Bad idea. First, think about why you're not taking the vacation. A lot of times, it's because you've told yourself that you have a position that nobody else can do. You've psyched yourself into believing that if you're not there, nobody else is going to fill in for you. That's only in your mind. Everybody is replaceable. If you're away, even for an extended period, somehow, your work is going to get done. If it doesn't get done when you come back, you're going to be stronger and clearer to complete it and faster because your mind is relaxed, and you know that it's going to make you better at what you do. The *pause* is such an important piece of getting respect.

Generally, in the middle, I'm telling you to pause now with everything, but you have to plan your pause.

The first thing about planning your pause is planning for all your excuses of what could go wrong, and planning an alternative time for your pause. What I recommend for your pause is that you plan seven full days where you can go somewhere. It doesn't have to be expensive. You can go where you're not going to be bothered.

But before you go, you'll need to set everything in place so that you can stop worrying. You're going to set things in place for your children, for your spouse, and for your job. You're going to plan your pause. You're going to tell as many people as possible that you're taking this pause and that is mandatory. Consider it "doctor's orders," since you're reading this book. I'm a doctor, and I'm ordering this for you. It's part of your prescription for wellness. You're going to tell the powers that be "my doctor orders that I must take some time off. Not vacation, but downtime."

Let's peek in on the life of my client, Sheila. Sheila is one of those types of women that has three jobs, sometimes four. She has a young son who's eight and a daughter who is eighteen. She is the rock of the rest of her family. When something happens to the extended family, the default response is "Call Sheila." Even when she's away at work and her husband and her kids are home, they don't call her husband, they call her. Sheila always picks up the phone and is always off to the rescue.

When I told Sheila to take a break, to take a pause, I knew it would be exceedingly difficult for her to grasp this concept. It was even hard for Sheila to step aside for forty-five-minute coaching sessions. It always seemed that something urgent would come up, and she would end up canceling sessions. We discussed taking just a one-day pause. I said, "Borrow the house of super friends. You know, go away to a cheap Airbnb or something. Someplace where you can go and be close to home, but be away from home." Sheila disappeared, and I got notes from Sheila about all the different, real crises that were happening in her family and in her life.

Why was Sheila fearful of taking a break? She didn't feel like she deserved it, and she enjoyed the feeling of being needed so much that somehow the universe always delivered a crisis, a real crisis, so that she could never take time for herself.

A crisis doesn't go on continuously. A crisis is finite and does come to an end. Even if someone is ill. Unless you're on the medical team taking care of that ill person in your family, there is always some time that you can hand off to someone else, if you have someone. You may say, "No, I can't leave the side of that person." I understand if that is your child, and he or she is under eighteen. However, even then, you must take a break. You must step away so that you can be better, even at times when you have a relative who's sick. You must put somebody else there so you can take a break. This is one of the biggest areas that people come up with where they would not take a pause. I get that and can go along with that. Again, these crises don't last all day every day, year upon year.

Let me tell you about Dr. Sydney and her pause, or I should say pauses. First, Dr. Sydney couldn't see herself taking off a week alone. But she ended up creating it as we talked about it. What happened after she came from that week? We had talked about taking a longer pause. She ended up with a paid family leave. She knew she needed a break, but she couldn't fathom how she was going to get the break she needed. Being the primary breadwinner in her family, it was a little frightening and, although she and her husband had planned financially for being able for her to make a transition, it was still scary to consider going away without the safety net of another job in place. When you put your mind to the idea, you are going to find a way to create the pause.

Sometimes, seemingly magical things happen. When I met Anna, she was already on a sabbatical from her college professor position. She had time to pay attention to her own wants, needs, and desires and had decided she wanted to understand herself better as we started working together. Three months after she enrolled in my coaching program, her sabbatical ended. At this point, as she was really grasping the methodology of The R.E.S.P.E.C.T. Method, she clearly understood why she needed to keep time in her life for her. We had incorporated a lot of specific discussion about her projector Human Design type and how this meant that she must stay vigilant about guarding her time and energy so that she did not burn out. She had experienced burnout in the past and simply chalked it up to a character flaw she felt she needed to correct. As a result of using The R.E.S.P.E.C.T. Method, Anna became very intentional about planning time. In addition, she would become grateful for the free days and times and began to say "no" more often to doing extra stuff for people just to be nice to them. Her friends and family were quite understanding and even told her that they were glad to see her slowing down and taking time for herself.

Often, friends and family knew that she was free on her sabbatical. They wanted to encroach on her time, but she learned to say "no." She learned to say, "No, I'm not going to go do that today." "No, I'm not going to go out to dinner." "No, I'm not going to go paint the apartment with Mom today." "I'm going to do exactly what I want to do." It always feels so good to do that.

One of the main keys to getting respected is self-reflection and releasing judgments of yourself. But for this to happen, you've got to have time and space. If you're saying, "I don't have any time and space," everyone needs time and space for themselves. It's your choosing not to respect your needs that makes it so hard to make time and space for yourself.

Now is the time to do it. We're in the middle of The R.E.S.P.E.C.T. Method. This is when the rubber meets the road. It's time for you to pause, reflect, and release.

How are we going to do this? A step that has been transformative with my clients is creating white space. It's a time where there's no agenda at all. It is time alone with themselves. The minimum is seven days, but I encourage a four-to-six-week period. But when you start carving out a seven-day period, it's not a time to go to a silent retreat. This is not a time to have a vacation with the girlfriends. Instead, this is a time for you to go to a hotel, or an Airbnb, or borrow a friend's house, and have no agenda, and to empty out your mind and spirit.

One of the reasons it's extremely hard to move forward in life and get what you want is because there's no space. There needs to be a space in you, in your energy, in your aura for all the things you want to come in. But first, you have to be able to let go of some of the junk that's in your head. During a pause is when you'll do this.

A lot of times, people say, "What do I do during this pause?" Here are some ideas. You're going to take along a journal. Now, we're going to talk about what you're allowed to do when you pause. Besides letting the world unfold in front of you, you will be able to make a quantum leap in your spiritual growth and in getting what you want through self-reflective journaling.

Have you seen the motivational poster featuring an iceberg? It's majestic. You see the tip of the iceberg peeking out of the water and the rest of it hiding beneath the surface. It's typically accompanied by texts like "success" or "imagination." The point is that you can only see a small section of it, but the work it took to create it is buried beneath the surface. You can think of your mind in the same terms as that iceberg.

The real driver of your mind is your subconscious. It is those habitual unintentional thoughts that drive your actions and behaviors. We think that we can control everything, but in reality, we struggle to control our minds. We are often on autopilot, and that drives us to take certain actions when faced with certain situations. Yet that action is not always the right one and it won't always result in the desired outcome. There's a good chance that you will do something and then question why you have done it that way, when there was a better way to deal with it.

We often behave in ways that sabotage our progress and act self-destructively. Do you know what can help this? It is *taking a pause and reflecting*. You can change how you view yourself and how you feel and act in certain circumstances. Therefore, through this pause and self-reflection, you can also shift others' perception of you.

WHAT IS SELF-REFLECTION?

Essentially, it is thinking about your beliefs and behaviors. To take it a little bit deeper, it's being honest with yourself when you dare to ask thought-provoking questions to bring out a deeper understanding of yourself.

What benefits does self-reflection offer to help you feel more at ease in your life, and lead to getting more respect and appreciation?

There are several. The greatest and most obvious benefit is that you will get to know yourself better. When you feel or act in a certain way, you can understand why self-reflection breeds awareness, which will allow you to become a more proactive person. When you think you're in control, you are. You will have a much clearer picture of who you are and what desires you hold.

You will have the competence and peace to overcome obstacles, and you can release emotional tension. Of course, there are indirect benefits of self-reflection as well, such as improved communication skills, social awareness, critical thinking, empathy, sensitivity, and tolerance. This will also have the long-term benefit of boosting your value, both professionally and personally.

Next, you're going to embark on a journey of self-reflection. It's important to point out there are two different levels you should aim to achieve regularly. The *first* is a bit of action retrospective, to improve yourself regularly and adjust your environment. The *second* is analyzing yourself to truly get to know yourself. There is always room for improvement to get reflective. No matter how successful or productive you already are in everything you do, there will always be a better way to do it. As your awareness grows, you become more willing to try new things and experiment. This allows you to improve your potential. As you grow wiser, you unlock your opportunity for growth.

Reflection, imitation, and experience. These three things are how we learn wisdom. According to Confucius, *reflection* is the noblest of these pursuits. You can start the self-reflection process by asking yourself these questions:

1. What went well?
2. What can I do differently next time?
3. How can I implement these steps/changes?

Once you answer these three questions, you can make a series of decisions.

Coaches often hand out sheets with these last three questions:

1. What will I start doing?
2. What will I stop doing?
3. What will I continue doing?

They give these questions to their bosses or colleagues and to their clients or employees. They get anonymous feedback about their performance, and they decide what changes they will make on the back of it. It's typically known as 360-degree feedback.

Perhaps if we were a bit more self-reflective and had any sense of self-awareness, we wouldn't need to hand others these sheets. Instead, we could easily fill them out ourselves. You can think of this as cutting out the middleman in order to know yourself. It's up to you how often you do these, but you should regularly schedule these intervals. Every seven days is a good choice, but you can try every fourteen days, if you like. This is where journaling flexes its muscles.

For your first self-reflection session, you will want to cast a critical eye on the preceding seven to fourteen days. This is the point where you will reflect on your actions and behaviors while also planning for the next week, to address the tasks you have completed in the last week, or to measure your progress on how you've moved yourself forward. This will allow you to plan and adjust your strategy. This is also your time to reflect on what you have learned, what new ideas you've gathered, and, of course, to set tasks for the week or two ahead.

Finally, as you journal along these lines, it's your opportunity to reconnect with yourself and ensure you are still connected to your "why." As you do this, it will allow you to identify areas for self-improvement. From all of that, you can answer these three final questions, on what you will stop doing, what you will start doing, and what you will continue to do. Always keep those in mind. You can journal daily. This is recommended during your pause.

Planned and intentional self-reflection should take place every ten to fourteen days for a deeper and meaningful look into yourself and to constantly reassess where you've come from, where you are, and where you want to go. This process is dynamic. You don't reflect once and that is it. Change will continue to happen in the world and in your life; therefore, you will have to adjust to current circumstances. What you'll notice once you get started is that the daily practice of journaling encourages self-reflection naturally.

BOOST YOUR SELF-REFLECTION VIA JOURNALING

Let's take a deeper look at the journaling process and self-analysis. Self-analysis is simply taking your self-reflection to the next level. For optimal results, we'll want to make use of both tools.

The biggest difference between the tools is that, when following self-analysis, there is no decision to make; it's simply about understanding yourself and recognizing without judgment. You shouldn't feel forced into a decision. It isn't about what you should stop, store, or continue to do. Instead, it's about impacting your life course by understanding who you are. It's much deeper, and it goes beyond planning. It's all about you, who you are, what you want from life, where you want to go, and who you want to be. You can learn how to cope with the emotions that are tripping you up in the behaviors you hate and increase your self-respect while you're at it.

Self-analysis will also influence your productivity, performance, and success, though more in the long-term as opposed to the short-term. It's fair to say that action retrospective includes your short-term performance and helps you build for the future. Self-analysis is more of a long-term function. The reason for this is that action retrospective focuses on *what* and *how,* whereas the self-analysis aspect of self-reflection is why.

You can approach self-analysis in two different ways. There is the cycle analysis method, which is valuable but time-consuming and costly. Or you can take this journaling path, the self-reflective journal. Your journal is going to be your tool for analyzing and reflecting.

Let's be clear: this doesn't mean you have to sit down and write about everything that happened today. Rather, you're going to write about how you felt when certain things happened, why they may have happened, and why you felt that way. You're going to think about how these feelings are linked to your beliefs and values. It isn't about what happened but what you thought, how you felt, your perspective, your environment, words, and actions.

The purpose of keeping a journal is to improve your self-awareness. You are reflecting on the day, the week, and the month and getting a clearer picture of your desires, your weaknesses, your whole self. It invites insight, and it nurtures understanding.

As you journal and regularly reflect, you will notice several things going on. You will get to know yourself as you are, in a variety of situations that life throws at you. You will become better connected to your desires, emotions, values, and ultimately your true self.

Your self-awareness will grow. Through environmental awareness, you will better understand the people in your life as well. You will develop your relationships by improving your capacity for empathy and love. You will become a more tolerant person, both to yourself and others. Your focus and clarity will improve. Tracking your evolution as a person will help you accelerate your development and growth.

There are additional business benefits of journaling. Journaling helps you purge your mind of troubling thoughts and emotions. This provides you with stress relief, but also increases your potential for self-analysis and creativity. When you journal, it's a chance to gain insights that you would otherwise miss. You're tracking your thoughts and emotions and that is always going to unlock insights. Maintaining a journal will effectively help you grow as a problem solver.

There are a few things to bear in mind as you journal to self-reflection.

Be consistent.

Journaling is cathartic; it's easy to sit down and let it all go when you've had a difficult day. It's not as easy to be consistent with your journal when you're having a good day. This needs to become a habit. Carve out time for it daily, whether you do it right before bed or take time out after dinner. Schedule it in your calendar, if you have to. Once you have the journaling habit, you will find your mind slips into the state of self-reflection quicker and it's easier to be quiet.

Listen.

Find a place where you can be alone and shut out all distractions. Part of the self-reflection process is association, and this will always lead you to the core of the issue. However, distractions interrupt associations and will make it a fruitless endeavor.

Ask "why?"

Why is a key question to use to trigger your association flow. Don't be afraid to ask yourself "why" four hundred times if you have to. The purpose of this exercise is to get to the core. How many licks does it take to get to the center of a Tootsie Pop? As many as it takes. Ask yourself "why" as many times as it takes. There have been a surprising number of studies into the Tootsie Pop question, but they all came to a different conclusion. Our point stands, that asking "why" will help you gain insight into why you find yourself in a situation and why you feel a certain way when you do.

It's important that you learn to distinguish between emotions and your mind. They are connected, but you should recognize that your emotions should serve as a compass to lead you to insights about yourself. For example, you have a promotion offer on the table. Logically, it's an easy "yes," because the job comes with greater opportunity and a large pay increase. However, your emotions might not align with your logic. Those emotions should guide you to "why" that's the case.

Here's a good example of how to use the benefit. Describe a situation that you have experienced. How did that situation make you feel? When you answer that, ask yourself again "why," and keep asking why until you can't ask why anymore.

Self-reflection isn't judgment. The purpose of journaling is to boost self-reflection and should not be to criticize yourself. Rather, it's to get a deeper understanding of yourself to gain insights and recognize tolerance. It's the opposite of criticism.

Self-reflection should increase your capacity for love, both toward yourself and toward others. Self-reflection should be honest, but it should also be gentle. Start your journal. The journal will be your go-to for reflection on both the bad and good experiences you have. It's all about learning from the experience. It will help you identify areas of growth and help you analyze yourself and the events that occur to you. You can write about your career, life, and relationships. There are several reasons you should journal to boost self-reflection. It will help you understand things and reflect on why they happen.

Align your actions with the lessons you're learning as well as your values, and allow yourself a space to vent. It's possible to reflect on an action while it's happening. This is teaching you how to think on your feet and problem-solve quickly. Reflecting on action is what we do once the event has passed. We stand on the outside of the event looking in, but step into the experience to access our memories and emotions on the matter.

When you write in your journal, think about what happened before the event, what happened during it, and what happened after the fact. Take yourself to the event in question. Think about what could happen, what might feel challenging about this situation or event, and how you can prepare for it.

During the event, observe what's happening, and ask yourself if it worked out as you expected. Did challenges arise? And did you deal with them appropriately? Is there anything you could say or do to steer the experience toward success? Following the experience, ask yourself how you felt immediately after it. Ask yourself again—when you've had time to put distance between the event and yourself—would you behave differently in a repeat performance? What can you learn from this experience? When you are writing reflectively, you should focus on what's next.

"What" is where you will recall the event in descriptive terms and record it. How did it happen? And who was involved? This is the interpretive stage, your opportunity to reflect on the event and interpret it for yourself. What was the most relevant, interesting, important part of the situation? How can you explain it? Is it similar to other events or completely different? What was the outcome?

This is where you come to a conclusion about what you can learn from the situation and how you can and will apply it to the next time this situation arises. Here are some self-reflective prompts to get you going on your journaling journey. These are all designed to trigger a bit of introspection that will help you in the endeavor of getting to know the real you. It's easy to get caught up in expectations and perceptions of everyone else and lose sight of what we want in life. Journaling to boost self-reflection is an excellent way to correct your path.

Ask yourself:

- "What makes me unique?"
- "Who is someone that means the world to me?"
- "What can I focus on to improve my health?"
- "What makes me smile?"
- "When do I feel most at peace?"
- "What does living authentically mean to me?"
- "What's my favorite animal?"
- "How can I maintain my health physically, mentally, and spiritually?"
- "What will I achieve this week?"

Write a list of five to ten items.

The most important advice I can offer you as you begin the journaling process is to always be honest. Don't use your journal to create an echo chamber. Use it to challenge yourself. To truly challenge yourself, you must be honest and focus on how you can progress in life. Don't just write reflexively as you do when someone asks you how you are—you automatically say "fine" whether it's true or not. That's not what your journal is for. There should be a difference between the questions you ask yourself daily and those you ask weekly.

The purpose of these questions is to help assess your progress and highlight areas you should focus on. This will help you find and fix recurring problems.

Ask yourself daily:

- "What good did I spread today?"
- "How was my energy today?"
- "How were my emotions today?"
- "In what directions did my thoughts guide me today?"
- "What did today teach me?"
- "Did I make a new decision today? What expectation do I anticipate from it?"
- "How did I treat myself and others today?"
- "Did any of my character flaws show their face today?"
- "Am I completely engaged or trapped in a KO routine?"
- "Did I push myself too hard today?"
- "Did I push myself hard enough today?"

This is a good opportunity for you to plan for tomorrow. Where will you need to channel your energy and focus tomorrow?

Try to limit yourself to three key tasks.

Reflect weekly:

- "Am I stronger than I was at the start of the week or am I weaker?"
- "What kind of person have I been this week?"
- "Am I trying to be someone else or pursuing myself?"
- "What character flaws have surfaced this week?"
- "What will I do about it next week?"
- "Where am I socially, financially, health-wise, romantically?"
- "Am I moving in the right direction compared to where I want to be?"
- "Why am I pursuing the goals I have?"

- "What are my top priorities?" (No more than five.)
- "What went well this week?"
- "What didn't go well this week?"
- "Are there any recurring issues I need to fix?"

You can finish these weekly reflections sessions by looking at how you have progressed with your goals, whatever they may be. Make it your mission to write in your journal daily before 9 p.m. You don't want to wind yourself up before bed, nor do you want to risk allowing too much time to pass between the experiences and emotions of the day and when you record them. I have included a multitude of prompts throughout this piece to help you get started. Often the most difficult part of journaling is getting started.

Learn how to say no to others and yes to yourself. Review your wants, needs, and desires often. Plan when you're going to take your next pause. When you pause, you can relax and release judgment. First, release judgment about yourself and your past. When you're able to release judgment about yourself, you also will notice that you become less judgmental about the rest of the world. As you pause and relax, empty out into your journal. Take a break, sleep, walk in nature, and eat well.

When questions or thoughts come in your head, do a journaling inquiry. Ask yourself "why" at least six times and after you finish journaling. Then pause.

8

ELEVATE YOUR ENERGY

Now that you've taken a little break, you can explore an area that will require your full attention and high amounts of energy and willpower.

ADDICTION TO PERFECTION

The addiction to being perfect is rooted in caring more about what other people think than about what your own thoughts and feelings are. At some point in your life, you made the choice to believe that other people's opinions are more important than your own, even when they are about you. These thought patterns led you to always be performing for someone else. As with any performance, you want to do it perfectly, and you loathe making any mistakes because a perfect performance leads to accolades and applause. You constantly seek the positive feedback and acceptance from those outside of you, and you begin to do practically anything, even when it goes against your own wants, needs, and desires, to get the accolades.

I've termed this desire for perfectionism an addiction because it causes dysfunction in your life, and it is not easy to get rid of at all. The emotions of getting over this addiction are circular because you will have anguish when you slip back into the behavior. You will first have an inkling of self-loathing that you messed up, and a perfectionist cannot stand messing up, even on the first try. Perfection addiction is like all the rest. It's so hard to let go because you cannot fathom who you would be if you aren't that perfect little girl. You don't know if you will like You, but more importantly, you are sick with worry that no one else will like you.

Your whole life and persona are built on Miss Goody Two Shoes. You don't smoke. You don't drink (or you have limited yourself severely with the utmost discipline). You don't overeat. You don't gamble. You don't do drugs. Wild reckless sex and sexually suggestive clothes are things you would never consider. You don't do any of those things that are outwardly frowned upon and that you've been brainwashed into believing are the downfall of society. You feel good about yourself because you've barely done anything remotely edgy. Isn't that why you look in the mirror at your post-baby belly and beat yourself up? You see that bulge in your middle as a sign of not having enough discipline or mental fortitude to get rid of it. You feel it is a sign of a character flaw rather than a badge of honor for being chosen to birth a child and to contribute to the continuance of humankind.

You feel utterly shattered when you get criticism from other people. You feel utterly shattered in your relationship when your partner doesn't see things the way you see them or doesn't appreciate you. This all began because this is about taking radical responsibility. Your fear of abandonment led you to do what you thought other people wanted you to do rather than doing the right thing that felt good to you.

I could lie to you and tell you this is going to be easy. In fact, that is what's written in lots of books. Just do this and it will be gone in an instant. The truth is that it's going to take a lot for you to get past this one, and it's going to be an everyday task of examining your thoughts, words, and actions. For you to get all the way there, you're going to need to have a strong team. These people can include colleagues at work who have proven to be allies. In addition, you will require coaches who will hold you accountable, help you bounce around your thought processes, and be honest with you if and when your perfectionist thinking is creeping back in.

Dr. Sydney was able to identify a colleague at work who could be her advocate, and one mentor at work, whom she had always gone to, had a high position in her hospital system. She knew that she could go to these people and bounce her ideas off them, and they would be willing to help her achieve her goals.

Acknowledge and be OK with the fact that most people aren't going to fall into your camp of allies for getting you what you want. Most of the time, they will fall into the camp of people who trigger your addiction because when you feed that addiction, you are acting the way they want you to act and in a way that serves their purpose.

That's a nice way to say that they don't care about you and are not thinking about your needs. When you identify those people, accept that they are the way they are and that you cannot change them. You need to step back and focus on what's going to serve you best to elevate your energy. You're going to let go of those people like that supervisor at work who was bugging Dr. Sydney. And sometimes the strategy is not to even engage with them.

For Anna, her quest to figure out the best way forward after the sudden end of her long-term romantic partnership has been a constant challenge for her. Some days she's up, and some days she's down. She would realize, when she was down, that her inner dialogue was all about what her ex-romantic partner was doing, thinking, and feeling. During those down times, she would be thinking, if she could just make him understand, instead of working on understanding herself, and how the whole situation was created in the first place.

Anna continued to work on refocusing herself through our coaching. It was always in my assignments for her to think about her own thinking, as opposed to the thinking of her ex-partner. The challenge with broken romantic partnerships is knowing that, at one time, your perfectionism was good enough to keep the relationship going. Now you're upset with yourself and questioning every move you made. You are resentful toward your ex-partner because you worked so hard at doing everything "right" yet it was still not appreciated.

I think it's exceedingly difficult, with romantic relationships, to let go of the notion that you can make somebody think and feel differently about you. We love someone until they act in a way that doesn't seem to serve us, but that serves only them. And, although they've been the same way all along, we still think that, somehow—after their pattern of behavior, in an instance, weeks, or months, in a sentence or a therapy session—that we're still going to change their thinking and their ideas. This is the nudge off the cliff of perfectionism you need, so that you can finally soar free.

Open your eyes, look straight in the mirror, and take radical responsibility. The only person you can change is yourself. Change doesn't come easily. Change comes as you develop new habits of thinking and being. Change comes from replacing what doesn't work.

How do you know your addiction is not the right way? The job isn't going the right way, or the relationship is gone. Letting go of the addiction means letting go of old habits, some of which may be lifelong. Others may have gotten you a few good things. Still others may be celebrated traits in your family or culture.

As you go through the rest of this chapter, where we explore exercises about how to stop caring what other people think, plan to return to this again and again. Highlight and bookmark this chapter. You will have to periodically check yourself to see how you're doing. You'll know when you're there because you'll have established clear boundaries that you will not let people cross. It will be a rare occurrence when someone tries to cross the boundaries.

In the beginning, you'll need to hold up those boundaries. It's going to feel like you are Atlas, the mythical Greek god burdened with holding up the world. After doing the spiritual exercises, your muscles will be strong, and your energy will be such that people will know they just can't get away with certain things with you. You won't even have to tell them, whether they're your bosses, colleagues, romantic partners, friends, or family.

An emotion that can be hard to get over is the feeling of being taken advantage of and letting go of resentment. You'll realize that resentment built up in you every time you said "yes" to things that you should have said "no" to. Now it's time for you to let go of some of that resentment. To do that, you must look at yourself. Other people can't change you; it is only you who can change yourself. When you blame others, you're not taking responsibility for your life. One of the biggest issues people face is caring more about what other people think of them than what they think of themselves. Once you learn to stop caring about what other people think, you're on a path to full self-respect. Let's talk about how you stop caring about what other people think. To feel a sense of belonging and acceptance is part of the human condition.

Most of us want to be liked and admired. However, sometimes these needs become unhealthy as they take center stage, and we can care more about what others might think. We may live our lives and choose our clothes, our words, and our point of view based on others' opinions. As we carefully wade through life under the control of a giant, judging, pointing finger, we become people pleasers and put others' opinions first before our own.

Some of you have lost touch with your own opinions, beliefs, and convictions. Maybe you were never in touch with them to begin with. You feel anxious and concerned as you worry about what they think about your clothes, your hair, or your opinion. Shame, embarrassment, and a deep sense of anxiety to your vulnerability bruise deep within.

For some of you, this condition began at a young age where a critical parent started pointing fingers at your ways, and it has stayed with you through your adult years. In this type of household, it is virtually impossible to develop a sense of self. Impossible standards, criticism, and abuse molds you as a child to become what others expect instead of allowing for the development of your sense of self. Maybe you simply don't know why you care so much about what others think. Perhaps insecurity and a lack of confidence motivate you to seek approval from others, even strangers on the street.

Whatever the reasons, many people are guilty of worrying too much about what others think. These perceptions are often overestimated. One study, *"Do others judge us as harshly as we think? Overestimating the impact of our failures, shortcomings, and mishaps"* (Savitsky, et al.), found that when people suffer an embarrassing blunder, social mishap, or public failure, they often feel that their image has been severely tarnished in the eyes of others.

Four studies demonstrate that these fears are commonly exaggerated. Actors imagined committing one of the several social blunders in these studies. The first study included those who experienced a public intellectual failure. The next two studies included those who were described in an embarrassing way. The fourth study was of those who anticipated being judged more harshly by others than they were.

Unfortunately, the irony behind the concern or obsession with what others think of us starts out as an effort to please ourselves in order to gain acceptance. But it does the exact opposite. Judgmental people will always judge, no matter how hard you try to please them. You can never be truly happy living your life from the position of what others want from you, or especially what you think they want from you. How many times have you changed your outfit before going to a party because, when you looked in the mirror, you were not looking at yourself through your eyes, but your mother's, your sister's, or your best friend's?

Being well-balanced in our relationships with others and how we affect the people in our lives is important. Too much concern about what they think is self-defeating. You value what others want or expect from you instead of living a life that is true to yourself and meets your needs. As we base our lives on our decisions and behaviors, on our expectation of how other people may perceive us, we don't do what we want to do. When you project what others will think, it's like living in a prison cell where all your movements are controlled by the prison guard. An imaginary judgmental finger is always pointing your way and controlling your movements, thoughts, and decisions.

It's time to break free and stop caring about what other people think. The truth is that, if you are living your life based on what other people think, you are not being true to yourself, and you are, in essence, living a fake life. How sad is that? You only get one life. Don't you want it to be your own?

To stop self-defeating behavior, you must stop pleasing other people. You need a new mindset, a complete flip of the script that runs in your head. Instead of "What is she going to think?" or "He's going to say that," you must switch your focus to "I think, I say, and I believe." You must form a healthy relationship with yourself, your ideas, and your opinions. Gaining confidence in yourself can overcome the need to please others.

STOP CARING WHAT OTHER PEOPLE THINK

Quit worrying about what others think. Think about how ridiculous it is to care about some stranger on the street having an opinion of you. You've never seen them before, and you will never see them again. These are the opinions that are easiest to let go of, versus a critical parent, longtime friend, a boss, or someone else you are close to.

Here's a short exercise that can break the pattern. Put on an outfit that does not match at all—polka dot sweaters, striped pants, and purple sneakers—throw an orange wig on your head and take a stroll on a busy street. Put on your biggest fake smile and wave at people who stare, laugh, or point at you. Do your best to push aside all the feelings and panic that you may feel and just do it. Keep talking to yourself with positive statements such as "Who cares that they are laughing?" "Who cares that they are staring?" "What difference does it make to me? Their opinions are irrelevant." "I am confident in myself. I am being me." Keep doing it to desensitize yourself, fake it until you can take that walk without caring at all what others are thinking.

Stop wearing makeup to go out and exercise.

You can't please everyone, only yourself. It is fruitless to try to please everyone because you never will. There will always be someone, or more than just one someone, who does not like your hair, your dress, or your opinion. There will always be judgments. There is no possible way to read that, and you have no control over what they say or do. What you can control is whether you let it affect you and live your life based on your terms or if you continue to be an actor in your life.

Imagine the freedom of not giving a flying fig about what people think. It is like that jail cell door is opening and you're being freed. Imagine this for a moment. The cuffs are unlocked, the chains are off. And there you are, free. You can wear whatever you like. Do your hair as you like, say what is on your mind, live life on your terms. Be yourself all the time. We're not that special. We often place an inappropriate amount of importance on ourselves. But people have little time to worry about you. Many are either worried about what *you* think of *them* and their shortcomings or they are busy living their lives.

The concept of being constantly watched and judged becomes overinflated. In reality, only a few people care.

Get to know yourself. See and appreciate yourself through your own eyes. It's important to get to know yourself. Who are you? What do you like? What makes you happy? What's important to your life? What are your goals? What inspires you? What are your opinions? What would you do if you never had to worry about being judged by others? What are your values?

Now you must practice asking yourself these questions. In your journal, make a long list and keep adding to it as you continue to think about this. Once you get in touch with who you are and what matters to you, you will become much less obsessed with what other people think. To put it simply, you will have a life, and knowing your values will give you something real to stand up for. You will no longer succumb to peer pressure, and you will stop saying "yes" to everyone and everything just because that's what you think they want to hear.

Spend time alone. If you haven't done your pause yet, do a pause for at least seven days. One of the best ways to get in touch with who you are is to live life from a quiet standpoint and spend time alone. Introspection requires quiet space, and when you are by yourself in a quiet place, you can get in touch with yourself and with your deepest needs. Meditation is also effective.

Though walking alone and getting lost in yourself works, it can also make a worst-case list. Get into a quiet space and start brainstorming; write down the worst-case scenario regarding what others think and what is holding you back from being yourself and doing what you want to do. "What is the worst that can happen?" Write it out in detail.

For example, if you wear the red dress that you believe will not be liked by your sister, what will happen? If you should state political views that counter your friend's or brother's opinion, what will happen? If you go to the free weights section of the gym where all the male bodybuilders are, what will happen? What is the absolute worst thing that can happen if you do that? What intimidates you? What holds you back from doing the things you want to do? What stops you from stating your opinion? Do you think they will like you less? Will the world end? All these answers will give you a clear picture of what stops you from being real and doing what you want.

The truth is that judgmental and ignorant people in the world are jerks. Who cares about what they think or say? Would you allow them to dictate your life? If the people close to you stopped liking you because of the dress, or an opinion, or your hairstyle, are these the people you need to have in your life anyway? Probably not.

You can use the exercise in your daily life whenever you hesitate to be yourself. Ask yourself, again, "What is the worst that can happen?" Unravel the overblown and unrealistic fears that dwell in your head, bust them wide open, so you can face them.

Understand judgmental people. You know the old saying, "When you point a finger at someone, there are three more pointing back at you"? This is 100 percent true. Judgmental people who criticize and point fingers are not judging you but themselves. These are unhappy people with miserable lives, and their judgments and commentary are a reflection of themselves, not you.

You only get one life. You know that you can choose to be happy. You can choose to live your life. You can choose to say goodbye to negativity. You can choose you.

All of us are heading toward the same ending of our stories, which is death. This is a fact of life, which can be daunting, scary, and liberating. It puts things in perspective. Life is short. Why waste it caring what other people think? Would you rather be grateful on your deathbed that you lived a life that was true to yourself?

Learn from the masters, spend time and surround yourself with those who have mastered being themselves. Don't mind what other people think. Have you ever watched anyone speak their mind and not wavered, no matter how others reacted? Did you notice their confidence and conviction? They will show you how it's done time after time. You might be surprised to see the respect these people get for being honest and direct, even when others may disagree with their views. Notice how good they feel about living a life that is true, and then remove all negative and toxic sources from your life.

Toxic people breathe toxicity; they are negative. Their negativity seeps into everything in their life and all who are around them. You know that person who always has something negative to say, some nasty, hateful comment to make about someone or something. These people will take you down, and you usually dread being around them.

It's time to let them go immediately. Clean out your phone contacts. The truth is that you cannot make anyone stop being mean, hateful, or negative. You certainly control whether they are or they are not in your life.

Make a trust list of the people who are most important to you. There are certain opinions that you will and should care about, especially concerning competences when seeking advice. The people who are on your trust list should be those who are loving, kind, and supportive of you and have your best interests in mind. They don't judge or criticize. We all need people to talk to, so keep the list handy and refer to them often.

The second list should be your "I don't give a crap what they think" list. Start this list with strangers, then add acquaintances and others. It is liberating to break free from caring what others think.

Stop chasing the irrelevant. Are you always chasing after those who don't like you? This is a typical dysfunction in humanity, as so many of us want to be liked. Instead of being concerned with those who don't like you and what you can't have, spend your energy and time on yourself so you can be the best you, not only for yourself, but for those who like you.

Have you ever stopped to wonder why you expect people to think bad things about you? We care about what other people think because we often expect something negative coming from them. This can be an indicator of how you feel about yourself and your insecurities. We may also assume the worst, and completely block out the good in various situations, while only paying attention to the bad. Pay attention to your thought process. Remove the negative to favor the positive. For example, instead of saying, "Oh God, they're going to think I look fat in this dress," say, "Wow, I'm going to wow them with this dress, I look great." At first, this will be difficult, and you won't believe it. But in time, with repetition, it will become a habit and you will believe it.

Perfectionists believe being perfect means being admired. First, no one is perfect and never will be. Second, it's exhausting to believe this. You're better off spending that time and energy getting in touch with yourself. Stop being an actor in your life.

No matter what you do in life, you will never truly escape vulnerability. This is especially true when you put your real self out there and let go of what others think. While you risk being vulnerable, the rewards of this freedom, of letting go, are plentiful. Be a friend to yourself. When you live your life from the standpoint of worry and anxiety at what others think, you aren't practicing self-nurture or being a friend to yourself. In fact, in many ways, this is not only self-defeating, it's also self-abusing.

The pressure and the shame associated with this cycle is certainly not anything that serves you. Consider this: if you saw a friend that you love treating herself or himself this way, would you be compelled to intervene? If so, be ready for confrontation.

Maybe the most difficult part in making this change is the actual interaction you might have with people as a result. Consider that when you always say yes or agree with others, it might be because you worry so much that they won't like you or will be upset with you. Once you accept that, there will be conflict that you will have to face.

For example, you were at lunch with a friend where she commented on some controversy and you don't agree; you think something totally different. For once, you speak up and state your opinion, and she reacts negatively. Perhaps she gets irked that you don't agree or she berates your opinion. (By the way, this is a good test of whether this is a person to have or not have in your life.) Or perhaps you go into that old panic: "Oh no, she's not going to like this." This will happen and you must be ready for it. If you can, role-play all possible scenarios with a trusted person so you can get comfortable being in that moment.

Plan and practice how you will hold your ground. Don't worry if you waver or make mistakes, such as succumbing to the pressure of agreeing. Stating and sticking with your opinion is more difficult than just worrying about people liking your dress or your hairdo. The main point is that you pick yourself up and keep going. When you do flop back to old habits, you will feel disappointed and let down with yourself. Use these feelings to keep moving forward. Notice how bad it feels. It will likely make you angry with yourself. Use these feelings to do better next time. They can be powerful motivators.

If all this seems like too much, or you find yourself struggling, then get help. A coach or therapist can help you work through any roadblocks you may face to reveal the real you. This can be helpful especially if childhood trauma blocks the pain of freeing yourself from the chains of worrying about other people's judgments.

Reaching out for help is well worth it to end the vicious cycle of suffering. Put yourself first. Put yourself out there. Put your *real* self out there, as this is the ideal way to acclimate yourself to a whole new mindset. This can be scary, but you can do it.

Put the above steps and all that you have learned into action. Be real, be honest, be your real self, face the world head on, forgive any slips, and keep pushing forward. You only get one life, so make it your own. The more you practice your newfound freedom, the more confidence you will gain as you focus on those who appreciate you, instead of worrying and focusing on what others think. With time, you'll find it easier to do. As you'll see, the sky will not fall when you are your real self, and you'll feel empowered and proud.

Remember, you only have one life. Don't you want it to be your own? When you stop caring what other people think, you'll be able to elevate your energy.

9

COMMIT TO YOUR VALUES

Have you ever wondered what your values are and how to put them into words? It's been an intense time all over the world: You've lived through the 2020 pandemic, the American presidential election, and the social unrest. It's been a clash of values. If someone has ever done something around you or to you that makes you upset, you feel like you can't even stand it. It makes you want to yell, scream, and holler. Or you just want to fix it and make them look, think, and act like you.

You're bumping up against their values, which are bumping up against your values. When you allow some boundaries to be crossed, you feel like you've been seriously violated. But there are other boundaries where something—you might not know what it is—just doesn't quite fit right with you. But by knowing what your values are, in your life and in your relationships, you can be true to yourself.

Humans are social animals. We thrive with others, especially people who are like us. We're always looking to be around people whom we can call our tribe, who share similar values. The way to make sure you're in the right place and in the right relationships is to verbalize what your values are and know what they look like in action.

As you move through this step of The R.E.S.P.E.C.T. Method, remember to examine the five areas of life:

1. health
2. wealth
3. relationships
4. career or life purpose
5. spiritual and personal development

In all these areas, you have certain ways of thinking and being that feel right for you.

A prime example of two values that seemed to bump up against each other became apparent during the covid pandemic. Protect health or protect freedom and wealth? What came first and foremost for you? People on each side of this debate were willing to fight and go to jail over this. One side could not understand the other side, and neither side was willing to change because beliefs in their values were that strong.

You cannot understand yourself as a person unless you consider every part of you, the physical, the emotional, and the spiritual. What are your values and beliefs? How do they align with the five key areas of life as noted above?

Determining which of those five areas is right for you will help you in creating your boundaries.

BOUNDARIES

The word boundaries is thrown around all the time. We have not yet defined boundaries, so let's do that and then go through an exercise so you can determine what your most important values are. Once you put words to them, they'll become clearer to you. Then, when you're faced with a crossing of boundaries, you'll know what works or doesn't work for you. You'll know your own values, attitudes, and beliefs. The more you know about yourself, the more questions and answers will come from your investigation.

Think about the things that make you an individual. What are your characteristics? What are your motivations? Your attitude is the mentality you have in response to certain circumstances, objects, or context clues. It can change wildly, easily, and frequently depending on your experiences. It is about what has influenced you daily and can be altered based on dislikes, likes, and interests. While you can learn a lot about someone based on their attitude, it's nothing like what their beliefs will show you.

A belief is simply an idea that comes from an experience or conviction. Your beliefs do not necessarily stem from fact, and they are not always logical. They are a reference point that allow us to interpret the world.

Values are your core ideals. They are what you consider right or wrong, or what's floating in a gray area. Values revolve around self-image and what makes you who you are. Values, like beliefs, are not necessarily logical, rational, or factual. In fact, your values are more difficult to change than your beliefs.

When you are sticking with your values, you operate as your highest self. Your highest self is essentially you in your purest form. You are truly meant to be aligned with a deep understanding of yourself. Your inner self possesses a great knowledge, a source of wisdom, that's there for you to tap into. You have layers; you are more than just your physical self; you are more than just your psychological self. You are a body, mind, and spirit, and you should take action to get to know yourself in each of these levels.

Let's first go through an affirmation to get us in the state of mind to be able to define our values.

'I TAKE CARE OF MY NEEDS FIRST' AFFIRMATION

- I ensure that my needs are taken care of prior to assisting others.
- I am mindful of my boundaries.
- I know where I end and others begin, I am conscious of my personal space, I respect the space of others, and I respect my

space.
- I protect my feelings and embrace my emotional security.
- I know that I need to take care of my needs before I can be there fully to take care of others.
- I honor myself, and I honor others.
- I fill up my cup first and then give from the overflow.
- I speak my truth in a way that is kind to myself and others.
- I am poised under fire.
- I adopt personal safety practices that feel right for me while also being mindful of others.
- I am self-compassionate.

Right now, take a pause to let those words of affirmation sink in. Get up. Walk around. Ponder what it feels like to embody this affirmation.

WORKING THROUGH YOUR VALUES

Below, you will find a list of values and their definitions. Pick the five most important values as your core values. Consider that these are convictions that you hold true for yourself. Realize that you look through a lens and hold other people to these same values. When you seem to get along well with someone, many times it's because your values align with them.

Value definitions

- **Accepting:** You are open to the values of others and of your own.
- **Aspiring:** You actively seek opportunity and focus on striving for success.
- **Authentic:** You are honest, genuine, and true to yourself.
- **Affectionate:** The ability to display and express strong feelings and love for others.
- **Assertiveness:** You stand up for yourself respectfully and know how to balance both your needs and the needs of others.

- **Compassionate:** You recognize suffering and alleviate it, whether it's your pain or someone else's.
- **Caring:** You are considerate.
- **Curious:** You are open-minded and interested in learning new approaches.
- **Challenging:** You consistently stretch yourself to try to improve.
- **Conforming:** You are respectful of rules and obligations.
- **Creative:** You are innovative, resourceful, and imaginative.
- **Courageous:** You are persistent and brave in the face of a threat, difficulty, or fear.
- **Emotionally aware:** You are open to your feelings. You are receptive to others' feelings.
- **Fairness:** You are reasonable, rational, and just.
- **Forgiving:** You can let go of negative feelings and don't hold grudges.
- **Gracious:** You appreciate what life has given you.
- **Honesty:** You are sincere with others and truthful with yourself.
- **Humor:** You love to engage in the funny side of life.
- **Industrious:** You are productive and hardworking.
- **Organized:** You are prepared, orderly, and organized.
- **Patient:** You can wait calmly for what you need or want.
- **Respectful:** You are considerate and polite.
- **Self-aware:** You are aware of your actions, feelings, and emotions, and of how others perceive you.
- **Tenacious:** You are persistent no matter what life throws at you.
- **Trusted:** You are loyal, reliable, discreet, sincere, and faithful.

Again, read all the values.

Pick your top five. Knowing your values will aid you in your life journey. Make a note of them.

Realize that, many times, your values inform your wants, needs, and desires. Make it a value to ask for what you want and be direct. Give only what you can without resentment. Do not expect others to live by your top five values. Everyone is entitled to choose their values. You just chose yours. Give other people the respect to choose their own values and accept that they are what they are.

10

TRUST AND TAKE ACTION

Trusting and taking action allow you to set yourself up for success after you've completed the first six steps of The R.E.S.P.E.C.T. Method. This final step is where the rubber meets the road. This is the time to decide what you truly think and believe.

Do you believe that all the work that you've done in spiritual transformation can result in getting the respect and the appreciation you deserve? Or do you believe that your task is to continue to try to change other people? Are you going to trust the process that you just read through, or are you going to go back to your old ways?

This is where you get the pep talk to understand that what you've done in the past is the reason for the way your life is today.

You've read this far because everything is not exactly how you want it to be. Your job and career may not be exactly how you want them to be. Your relationships, especially your romantic relationships, may not be exactly how you want them to be. You've taken radical responsibility at this point to admit to yourself that your thinking created certain actions, which created certain results.

This final step is about putting new thoughts and intentions in front of you and taking the proper steps to make sure that what you want—such as respect in your career or respect in your relationships—comes to fruition.

Radical responsibility requires working on yourself, by going through the steps, honoring your unique spiritual design, and mastering the steps to be completely and spiritually mature. This is where magic and miracles seem to happen. This is the step where, if you follow religion, you pray and leave it in God's hands. For those who are spiritual, you release it to the creator of all there is, into the universe, and allow the universal laws (that no one ever tells you about) to work.

No matter what spiritual type you are, this step requires patience. Some people are just built to be able to trust and believe easier than others. And so, they're able to manifest their desires faster because, once they set their mind to it, and once they know that there's a different way to do it, they simply trust enough to go about doing it.

That was the case for Dr. Sydney. We worked together for three months. She had major shifts in her life, from crying and being bullied at work, and not having the time she wanted with her husband and young child. She was working long hours, not being appreciated in her area of expertise, and not having the time to pursue the path she wanted to pursue.

Within ten weeks, she made major changes in her job situation, because she followed closely and trusted the process. She took three months of time off with full pay. This time off was something Dr. Sydney hesitated to even consider because, in that first session, she couldn't fathom how she could ever get something like this, given her unsupportive supervisor. As Dr. Sydney went through The R.E.S.P.E.C.T. Method, step by step from week to week, what she wanted, needed, and desired were offered to her. Her own doctor suggested the time off and wrote a letter. The HR department approved it within a day. Within a week of returning from her seven-day pause (which we planned for her during our session), she was again off from work and free to envision her best next step in life. She figured out how to lean into being a projector, wait for recognition, and get invited for exactly what she wanted—a paid sabbatical.

Anna was having a harder time in this area of waiting and patience. Her struggle was more about habit than anything else, as she was used to chasing after what she wanted. At times, she felt like waiting was doing nothing, so she'd let go and give up hope for what she wanted—her broken long-term relationship to be repaired. Anna felt that her heart was bursting with love and desire, and that she was no longer able to give it to him or receive it from him. It was sheer mental torture. For her, hope meant there must be something she could do or say to change her former boyfriend, to make him listen to her logic, to make him understand and agree to her reasoning why he should take her back. It was agony for Anna to stop the chase, tend to herself, and wait for an invitation or recognition. Accepting that the recognition and invitation may not come from this man was a painful realization, which brought her to tears during many of our coaching sessions.

Part of my coaching centered around helping Anna trust that leaning into her spiritual design was going to ultimately result in the best life for her. Of course, there was no guarantee that her last love was going to come back into her life. No matter what she did, whether it was running after him or sitting and waiting, there would be no guarantee. What did happen was, as Anna began to feel better about herself and work on herself, other types of opportunities became available for her that she may not have seen or taken before she did the work.

Previously, when she was aware of opportunities that didn't fit with her, she said "yes" when she should have said "no." She now had the courage to go back and say "no" to opportunities she had committed to doing (for example, some side accounting for a company).

"This is not what I do best," she told me. "This is not even something I enjoy. I said yes to this just to be nice. I don't want to do this anymore. I'm going to go back and tell them no."

After she went back and told them "no," she realized that she didn't care what other people thought anymore. Suddenly, she was a lighter person who discovered that having more time and space for herself, without doing something out of obligation, was a good thing for her.

Anna was able to lift her mood and continue on her path. She also saw a therapist and learned both how to understand herself and to listen for understanding of her former partner. Her decision was now about accepting that, if her former lover came back into her life, he was going to be exactly the same design as he was before. Therefore, she must then be willing to take him exactly the way he was. His value system, which may not now or have ever fit with her own, would put his values and boundaries at the front of the relationship. She would need to decide how to draw the lines—*if* she wants to draw the lines. She could simply fall back into the pattern of being underappreciated and undervalued again.

This is the tough choice that many women must make in romantic relationships. Are you going to acquiescence to what he wants and live with resentment and regret? Or are you going to stick with your values and boundaries, get the respect and appreciation you crave and deserve, and thereby feel happy and fulfilled in the relationship?

How to Manifest

Up until now, you've been doing a lot of work on yourself. This work has involved being open to a lot of introspection and self-examination. Now it's time to consider all the listening that you've done, and trust that you're on your way in the right direction.

The difference between listening to yourself and hearing yourself is being active versus passive. When you hear something, you don't pay attention to it. If you've done all this work, and all this writing, and then you do nothing at all after it, you've only heard it. This is where I've seen people journal and write lists and build vision boards. They can have journals, lists, and vision boards up the wazoo, yet they're stuck in life because they didn't trust and take action. They just expected that, no matter what they did, things were just going to happen.

Part of getting what you want in life is trusting that it's going to happen and taking inspired action. You may feel a sense of discomfort and fear. That's a good thing. When there's discomfort, it means that growth is taking place. Of course, the first time you do something, your muscles are going to be weak and out of shape. You're not going to do it exactly right or well, and it will feel hard. Just like lifting weights, you've been defining thoughts, feelings, and your spiritual self. You've also been reflecting on what this all means and how you are going to move forward in life, now that you have this information.

The final piece is about putting in place a way that causes good things to fall into your lap, as situations and opportunities come your way.

You might have noticed, up to this point, if you've been doing the exercises and working along as you read this book, that your life has already changed in a discernible way. Even if you haven't done a whole lot, your energy has changed, and you've drawn some new and exciting people and opportunities to you. You might feel lucky—but luck is equal to manifestation.

Manifestation is an area that some people find a bit too woo-woo. Manifestation is the ability to think something into existence. Sounds crazy, right? But it can happen. It is real, and it happens every day. Once you learn the power of this process, you can use it to achieve your goals and bring your dreams into reality. Your thoughts, your feelings, and your beliefs can be used to manifest something you want into physical reality. But you must know how to do this work.

There are three pillars of manifestation that are easy to remember: being, doing, and having.

Being

The first pillar is about being the person you are striving to be. It is about learning to inhabit the beliefs and choices of a person who deserves happiness, who can achieve their goals, and who is committed to realizing their objectives. Before you can do something, you must have the right outlook or mindset that will get you the results you want. In other words, it is not enough to act a certain way or to want something. You have to embody the values, beliefs, and thoughts that are needed to realize your dream.

Doing

Everything you want in life requires something from you. It may require learning action, a change in circumstances, new choices or habits, or a change in your outlook. If you need to adjust your mindset, you must be willing to put in the work to do that. If you need to learn some new skills, you must put in the effort. If you should adopt healthier or more productive habits, you must take the necessary action to develop these.

Action is not always easy, which is why you must rely on being the right type of person, having the right mindset to stay the course and perform the necessary actions. Doing does not just happen because you want it. It occurs when you make the conscious choice to behave, to move, to change, to learn. It requires effort.

Having

While realizing your goals may seem like the endpoint, or that having something is the ultimate result you seek to achieve, this is not necessarily true. When you have invested in the being and doing, having what you want should become a stepping stone to a new goal, the manifestation of something new in your life.

Having means you have realized something important to you, and that your journey is ready to continue in a new direction. It is time to circle back around to *being*, to achieve your new dream and begin the work of *doing* to attain it. *Having* also means handling your newfound happiness well, sharing it with others, putting your gratitude out into the universe, and acknowledging the work that went into its fruition. Without these actions, you can take your achievement for granted, you may lose sight of what is important to you, and you may struggle to be genuinely happy with your accomplishments.

How to Achieve Manifestation

There are nine steps to bringing what you want into reality.

Step 1: Examine your thoughts and feelings.

Getting a handle on your current mindset, emotion, outlet, and values is an essential part of the manifesting process. You've been doing this throughout your journey with this book. Are you feeling favorable toward the future? Do you often feel angry or upset? Do you value other people understanding your current beliefs? Understanding your current beliefs can help you identify those that could limit your success and keep you from manifesting what you most desire. Clear your mind of negative energy, work toward reconciling negative self-talk, and learn to treat yourself with more kindness and fairness. You'll realize that you've been doing this work all along throughout this book.

Step 2: Get clear about what you want.

Without a clear outcome, manifestation will feel like a lot of wasted effort. You need to know precisely what it is you want, including what that outcome will do to benefit your life once it is achieved. List the attributes of each of the things you are trying to manifest, being sure to focus on what is positive and desired about each. The more specific you are about what you want, the more likely you are to manifest something that matches that goal. Instead of saying "I want a new job," you might say, "I want a position that is 15 percent higher in salary than my current job, has similar or better benefits, and allows me to learn new skills while working with people who challenge me."

A vital component of achieving this clarity is giving yourself permission to change your mind in the future. Yes, you may want that new job today. But if things change where you currently are, then your goals or needs may change as well. That does not mean you failed to manifest it. It just means you need your needs to change. Give yourself permission in writing. Be specific about what the permission is and what it is for. Give yourself permission to change your mind.

Step 3: Ask for what you want.

Now that you are clear about what is essential and what you want in life, it is time to start asking for it.

There are many ways to ask the universe to help you realize your dreams. Best strategies for manifestation include visualization, meditation, creating a vision board, prayer, and positive affirmations. Realize that they are just a piece of the process. They are all activities that vocalize or solidify your intentions and needs, and they do it in a way that reminds you, and possibly others, of what is most important to you.

It is never enough to ask for what you want just once; you need to keep asking again and again, and you may need to ask in new and diverse ways. The more often you ask, the more energy you are devoting, and the sooner your manifestation will occur.

Step 4: Develop an action plan and start working.

When you work on manifesting something, you are cocreating your reality. The more effort and focus you give, the more likely you are to receive what you want.

Create an action plan that breaks down what you need to do to realize your goals. Write down three things you can do today that will help you get closer to your goal. Be inspired by others and look to them for guidance, if you are unsure what actions would help you realize your dreams.

The important thing is to commit to doing something daily. And the more you act, the more motivated you'll be to manifest what you want in life.

Step 5: Rely on your outlook to make the process work.

During the process of growth and change, you will experience setbacks and sometimes feel discouraged or frustrated about your progress. That is when your attitude, beliefs, and choices matter the most. Trusting in the manifestation process and believing that everything you are doing is for the best, will ensure that you are on the right path. When you experience setbacks or feel doubt, remind yourself that what you send out comes back to you.

Step 6: Acknowledge and celebrate what you receive.

Life, others, and the universe are always offering you help and guidance. Many opportunities come your way every day, but you must be willing to see them, acknowledge them, take advantage of them, and celebrate them with positivity.

The signs and possibilities that you get from the universe are a gift because you are ready to receive them. You must ensure that you are open and willing to accept them and remember to show gratitude for all the blessings that you receive. Gifts come in many different forms, and it is all in how you view them. Whether you believe this is manifestation at work, list your gifts and all you're grateful for.

Step 7: Check in with yourself.

To manifest something takes time, energy, and focus. Check in with yourself regularly and look for limiting beliefs. Changing your daily actions and evaluating your progress can help you achieve your goals.

Are you sending out the kind of energy you want to attract? Are your beliefs supporting your work or getting in your way? Are you paying attention to each of your choices?

Are you giving of yourself in positive ways to others? Are you mindful every day of being, doing, and having—the three pillars of manifestation?

The lesson from the three pillars is that merely doing any one of these will not result in a permanent change and the lasting happiness that you seek through manifestation. You must become the person necessary for achieving your goals. This will guide your actions, which will result in you having everything you want.

Step 8: Remain positive.

Keeping your energy positive and enthusiastic is the best way to promote manifestation in your life. If you want to attract good things, you must feel and project good things. Focus on what you want by asking for what you need. Spend time each day doing something that makes you feel motivated and positive. Focus on things that help you ask for what you want, and do the work that is necessary to accomplish your goals. Stay thankful and positive. Feel the joy of your dreams and desires. Push negative thoughts aside and focus on controlling your outlook and mindset.

Step 9: Get rid of limiting thoughts, beliefs, and actions.

Clear the universe of unhelpful thoughts and beliefs. Let go of negative and sabotaging behaviors. Stop resisting and learn to accept what you can't control. Feeling frustrated, anxious, or disappointed is a way of resisting. When you find yourself procrastinating or making excuses, you are resisting. When these things happen, acknowledge what is happening and ask why, answering and confronting these reasons. Confronting these reasons is a significant step to continuing on the positive path to get what you want. Ask yourself: what am I frustrated with or about? What am I resisting? Why am I resisting this process?

How to Quickly Get What You Want

Here are some ways for you to manifest more quickly to get what you want.

Avoid cynics and negative people.

One surefire way to sabotage your progress and interrupt your ability to manifest your goal is to listen to the cynics in your life. There will be people who say you can accomplish something by manifestation. There will be people who do not believe in you, who doubt your abilities or your intentions. They will try to stand in your way, block your success, and say you should give up. Do not allow naysayers and negative people to block your energy, to influence your choices, or to derail your efforts. Remember that you are trying to put out positivity in the world, which means wishing them healing and focusing on what is important to you. List negative people in your life and how you will deal with them.

Start from faith.

Whether religious or otherwise, faith is simply the belief in something intangible or what has not yet been shown to you. Faith is unwavering and continual. Even when things become unsure or pessimistic, trusting that it will work out and that you will soon realize your dream can keep you going, especially during setbacks and after plateaus in your progress. Faith helps you remain positive, keeps you focused on your outcomes, and allows you to surrender to the world when things are out of your hands and beyond your control. It is also what can help you overcome doubts, because you know deep within that good things are coming. You just have to be patient and keep doing the right thing. Reflect upon my trust and faith affirmations. For example, I trust myself, I trust the process of manifestation, and I have faith that all will work out.

Stop worrying.

In many ways, worry is a kind of resistance that can become counterproductive to your manifestation process. When you indulge in worry and anxiety, you allow yourself to consider the possibility of failure, to doubt yourself. You are telling the universe that you believe something bad is going to happen, that you do not think you deserve or will achieve success. When this happens, you will get back the same energy you send out.

Worry is a way of visualizing adverse outcomes. You imagine all the things that might go wrong. Worry influences all your thoughts and emotions. It even affects your body. You're sending these negative messages out, making you focus on what is wrong or could go wrong.

You're more likely to see problems than possibilities, which can lead to issues becoming realities. What are you worried about? How will you counter your worrying thoughts with all the positive possibilities and outcomes in your life or goals?

Build your self-confidence.

Believing in yourself and your abilities to realize your dreams is a crucial part of manifestation. It is part of the belief system that informs everything else. When you are struggling with self-worth, try creating an image of a successful you. Visualize yourself as happy and content. Imagine the You who has accomplished your goal. Actively explore this version of yourself in your mind and know that this version of you exists and is inside of you right now. Remind yourself often of your capabilities and accomplishments and acknowledge that you are worthy of the things you see. When you doubt, return to these exercises again and again until you genuinely believe in yourself. List all your accomplishments, achievements, victories, and capabilities in your journal.

Meditate regularly.

Meditation is a crucial practice that can help you focus, visualize, and attract the things you most want in life. Meditation is a practice of learning to focus your mind on one thing while pushing aside or ignoring competing thoughts, distractions, and negative influences. When you practice it regularly, at least once per day, meditation rewires your brain and makes you think differently. It changes your ability to pay attention by becoming more aware of thoughts that could derail your progress or those negative feelings you are projecting. You can adjust and change to improve your manifestation errors. Awareness is the first step toward transformation, and meditation is the perfect way to teach yourself to be more aware of yourself, your thoughts, your actions, and your feelings.

Read your action plan often.

Just as you must regularly repeat what it is you are seeking from the world, you must also continually review your action plan. The more you consider your plan, the more you embody what it is you are trying to become, and the more ownership you have over not only the effort, but also the outcome. Reviewing your plan can help you visualize yourself completing each step. Imagine the results of your hard work and put positive energy toward the steps that need to be taken to realize what you want.

Listen to your instincts.

Be aware that your intuition or instincts include your ability to know or understand something at once, without much conscious thought or basic reasoning. Your instincts direct your attention and focus and tell you deep down what you need to hear before you have much time to even process what is happening. In practice, your instincts are a manifestation of your values and beliefs. Those things you believe in your core that are most precious to you will trigger your intuition long before your rational mind has a chance to catch up.

Practice visualization.

There's a funny thing you may not know about your subconscious. If you create a mental picture of something, your brain believes it to be true. When you plant new ideas into your mind using visualization techniques and repeatedly showing these images, your subconscious believes these to be your reality. It will then work hard to continue to create the conditions to make this reality stay constant. This is why visualization works so well. You can plant new realities into your mind, and when you continue to practice the techniques, it will influence your emotions, thoughts, and actions over time. Create a mental picture of what you want and of the person you will be when you achieve it. How will you feel? What will be different about you and your life? The more you visualize this, the more likely it is to become a reality.

Send out what you want to receive.

When you're practicing manifestation, it is helpful to imagine the world around you as an echo chamber. Whatever you send out into the world through your voice, actions, or emotions comes back to you from many sources.

If you wish to find love, you must send out this feeling to receive it. If you wish to find respect, you must send out this feeling to receive it. If you wish to find appreciation, you must send out this feeling to receive it. If you want to see abundance in your life, spend time helping others find it in theirs. Give out what you seek to get back.

It is helpful to remember that the energy you send out may come back to you from unexpected sources or through a delayed response. For example, helping one specific person does not mean that you will receive help back from that same person. Instead, someone different may assist you some time from now. The point is not that you receive back the same action but that you get back the same energy and intention from the universe. Try it today. Send out a message of hope, peace, love, or whatever else you are trying to bring into your world and notice what starts happening soon.

Work on acceptance.

Accepting that manifestation works, that you can create your reality, and that you are in charge of your future, are perhaps some of the most challenging things for some people to do. If, for a long time, you've believed that life was getting in the way of your dreams or that you were not meant to have everything you want, accepting the power of manifestation can be incredibly difficult. Learning to accept that your fate is already in your hands and that you have been manifesting your life all along is a crucial step in your journey.

Focus on your needs.

To manifest what you most desire and need in life, it is critical that you focus only on what you want, and ignore what others tell you to wish for, or to think you should want for your life. Living your life for others will not result in happiness or contentment for you, and you must push aside their goals and agendas in favor of your own. When you find yourself listening to others, you are giving in to what they think is best for you. Ask yourself if they are the ones that must live with those consequences. Ultimately, it is your happiness alone that matters, not what anyone else thinks or wants for you.

Realize all that you have manifested and build from there.

When you become conscious of your ability to manifest your life, it can be helpful to take stock of all the ways you have already, perhaps unintentionally, created your current existence. Once you take stock of all the ways you have already manifested things in your life, you can see your real power. And once you become a conscious creator of your future, you can learn how to harness that power for good and to make better things happen for you in the future. What thoughts, beliefs, and energy have you sent out into the world to create your current reality? What choices have led you to where you are right now?

Support your dreams instead of ignoring what you want.

Start supporting your dreams in every way imaginable. Believe in yourself. Think positive thoughts about your possible outcomes. Put yourself in the path of opportunity and support your goals in every way you possibly can.

Direct your energy to become powerful and effortless.

You must be clear about what it is you want and focus as much as you possibly can on that singular goal. The more concentrated your energy and the purer your intentions, the more likely you are to yield a positive reward sooner. When you push aside all your other thoughts, worries, doubts, and fears and focus solely on this one thing, nothing can stop you from manifesting what you most want in this world.

Getting respect and appreciation is trusting and taking action in a way that manifestation can and will work.

11

HOW TO GET OUT OF THE QUICKSAND

We've already established that you are a perfectionist. You will be perfecting what you learn from now until the day you close your eyes and transition into that other time and space (this is a fancy way of saying "death").

However, there are elephant-in-the-room pitfalls that may seem obvious. Some are so simple that you will think to yourself, "Yeah, but how do I do that?" This thought pops into your head because you have been conditioned to believe that getting what you want is hard. Think back to geometry class. You might have really hated geometry, but the one concept that you probably remember is that the shortest distance between two points is a straight line. As you read this next section, keep this in the forefront of your thoughts and ask yourself, "Is this *being* said to help me make the straight line to exactly what I want?" Or you can also ask, "Am I doing things that are creating something other than a straight line?" Keep asking yourself, "Am I making this harder than it needs to be?" If the answer to this question is, "Yes," that's because you have decided that there is some benefit to you to not go in a straight line, such as, "I'm really scared of what other people will think, and it is easier for me to do it the way I am than to deal with the fear of not being accepted."

Since you are still reading, you are ready for the shortcut to getting the respect you deserve. Here are three simple steps.

1. Stop doing stuff that does not work.
2. Listen to people who have it together and have done what you want to do.
3. Show up to have accountability and get feedback.

Don't be lulled into believing that simply getting to the end of this book means that you have shown up. Showing up is about constant implementation of the concepts in this book. You will have dog-eared pages, you will have highlighted sections, there will be writing in the margins, and you will have started filling in a journal. Consider this book a textbook not unlike your college or professional school textbooks. To gain mastery, you must put in the time and effort just as much as you did your primary profession. You will need to become a student of your own storyline (and of all the excuses you use that keep you from getting respect and appreciation) so that what you've taken from this book can take effect. To really learn it so that you know it, to master these concepts, can only happen by getting feedback. Similar to the way you learned to drive a car and mastered it, you will have to be taught by someone so that you can more quickly correct errors to avoid accidents. That is what showing up is really all about: learning by doing and getting feedback.

What feedback am I talking about here? It's the feedback you'll get by taking part in coaching and mentoring and being diligent about participating in the sessions. This seems obvious; however, not participating in sessions is the most common way to avoid doing what you know you need to do, to get what you say you want. One of my recent clients, Sheila, completely went off the radar (i.e., disappeared) when she didn't want to or couldn't wrap her mind around taking off one whole day for herself.

Sheila, who has had multiple lifelong health problems (she started having weird problems around age nine and is now in her mid-fifties), enrolled in my coaching program because she had mystery illnesses. She did finally get one helpful answer; while we were working together, she was diagnosed by a Western-trained doctor with reflex dystrophy. However, the diagnosis did not alleviate the multiple issues she had, including an unspecified autoimmune disorder. Sheila began to work with me because she understood deep down that her physical problems were not only physical. What was probably scary for her was understanding the spiritual state (including her stress) that was triggering her health problems.

Here's how it went. We made a plan for how she would take one day off for herself, and we scheduled her next session after that day off, to debrief on how the day went. The morning of the session, Sheila sent a text to me apologizing that she can't make the session. Multiple "crises" had arisen in her family, and in her three jobs that meant she could not take a "free" day and couldn't even make a fifteen-minute laser coaching session. Four months later, she still had not rescheduled.

Sheila was hiding and *not* showing up for herself, because she had made the choice to show up for everyone and everything else. She couldn't even give herself fifteen minutes.

What was the message from Sheila's actions? "Hey, I'm just not ready right now to commit to changing." And that's cool by me. That is one reason why I offer a one-year laser coaching program. When Sheila is ready to come back for coaching, she can jump back in. That's how personal growth is at times. You start and it gets intense for you, so you stop and then, a few months later, you are ready again.

When you have those times when you don't feel like showing up, you don't have to show up. You know that you can do so in the future, before you're at the end of that coaching year. Get back on my coaching calendar, no judgment from me, and we'll celebrate your return.

To get change quickly, even when things are going crappy, even when you didn't do your homework, and even when you feel like you've been totally delinquent in your responsibility to yourself, you show up anyway.

Here's an example from my life. I decided to take on learning to speak French as a hobby, so I've been taking French classes privately. I love going to France. I feel at home there. My husband's primary language is French. His family lives in France, with an older brother and older sister in Paris, an older brother in Lyon, and his youngest sister near Poitiers. I would love the opportunity to live in the South of France, in a town near Nice or Monaco. Let me just tell you, French, for me, is hard. It's one of the most challenging pursuits that I've ever been involved in. In my opinion, it is much harder than going to medical school and becoming an eye surgeon. My mouth muscles as an American English speaker were not at all exercised to form French sounds. My ears were not trained to listen to French sounds. I often wonder why it's so hard for me, whereas, quite frankly, most of my pursuits have come pretty easily when I apply myself. When my French teacher gives me homework, I procrastinate or I do it really quickly, so I can get it out of the way and not have to think about it. French still makes my brain hurt.

You might be thinking, "Learning French is not life-altering, so why are you torturing yourself, Veronica?" I feel like I will have missed something in my life without having learned to speak another language, and I long to live at least part of my life outside America. My commitment to this is so important that I have gone three times to one-month immersion classes in France (where we can speak only French all the time). OMG, was it scary and hard! I am now considered advanced! What I am most proud of is that I made the commitment to myself, of both the time and the money, because I *want* this and for no other reason.

Back here in America for my weekly French lesson, sometimes I don't do the homework, and I feel guilty about myself, and want to just cancel the lesson. But I don't cancel the lesson. I show up on Zoom and Skype (yes, one of my teachers still uses Skype) anyway, completely unprepared. I am also honest with my teacher that I just couldn't muster up the desire to put down all the other stuff going on in my life to practice French. When I show up to the lesson, even though I didn't do my homework, I always learn something new, and I surprise myself and the teacher that I am able to speak or understand something I thought I could not.

The beauty of the situation with my French teacher, Angelique, is that she has herself done years and years of personal development work. So, when I have a crisis in another part of my life, and I want to make the excuse not to show up for that one hour and fifteen minutes, Angelique understands and can acknowledge, with grace and ease, that I am showing up when I don't want to be there. She realizes that this is just where I am at the moment, and she looks for ways to use French to help me move through life and on to all of my goals.

By the end of that seventy-five minutes, the energy has shifted upward because I took the time. That was *my* time. That was *my* pleasure that was seemingly frivolous, yet I progressed in French and in my spirit. This changes the flavor of the rest of the day to sweet from sour.

When I'm having a life crisis, Angelique is one of my coaches, not just in French but also in life. I also end up coaching Angelique through some of her life crises. I'm at the point now where I can say enough in French to converse and, with the help of Angelique and my dictionary next to me, I can explain some of the ins and outs of what is going on in my life, in rudimentary terms.

I almost forget about my crisis because I'm busy concentrating on speaking and understanding French.

OBSTACLES TO BECOMING APPRECIATED

Here are some other ways you can mess up while moving from being disrespected to being appreciated.

Mess up #1: Figuring it out on my own.

Depending on your IQ, this is a common mistake of high-performing people: They think, "I'm smart, I can figure this out on my own. I'll just read a book. I'll just watch a video. I'll do it all myself."

You started reading this book because you got to the point where you weren't getting respect. You didn't even know how it happened. Now you realize that it was your energy and your choices. You're still a high IQ and an intelligent person, yet you got yourself in this pickle. Don't depend on the letters behind your name to convince yourself that you got this all down. It takes work and practice to realize that you can have a high IQ but a low SQ—spiritual quotient—and end up in a situation where you're the doormat and not getting the respect you deserve.

Mess up #2: Not including your unique spiritual design.

The longest chapter in this book is about knowing yourself spiritually, because no one teaches us how to know who we truly and authentically are. There are multiple parts to that.

You've gotten to the point in life where you're an alert individual. Yet, a lot of times, you haven't felt comfortable in your spiritual walk and with your spiritual you. We all talk and say that we're mind/body/spirit, but we spend very little time on our spirit, outside of formalized religion where someone else is telling us what we should do and what's right for us.

The creator of all gave you a unique spiritual DNA, and you are the only person who can understand who you are, through self-examination. Any plan where you go forward, doing things that don't align with your unique spiritual you, is going to fail.

Mess up #3: Not accepting someone else's spiritual journey as theirs and not yours.

We often think that other people should have the same values as we do. In fact, many times, we can't even agree on what respect means. Your definition of respect is based on somebody who believes that your defined values are important. Have you realized now that you could be in a situation where your values aren't aligned? You need to accept that other people's values don't have to be aligned with yours. Choose situations where your values do align with your purpose and your relationships. Develop the courage to make different choices.

Mess up #4: Believing that the answer is to change others.

Do we need to say much more about this? You already know you cannot change others; you can only change yourself. If you're in a big social movement, you're going to work with others to figure out how to make systemic change. But on a micro level, you can only change yourself. And as you change yourself, other people around you also change.

Mess up #5: Not accepting that others have different realities and truths.

Your truth is only *your truth*. Your reality is only *your reality*. Someone else may experience the same events as you and interpret them completely differently. You choose your emotions, they choose their emotions, you choose your reaction, they choose their reaction. You give respect to others; they also give respect to others. They are also allowed to fully have their reality and their truth.

Mess up #6: Having self-sabotaging behavior.

There is a part of you actively working against you. This can literally be your greatest energy. It's the critical voice in your head, the one that denies you and sends you negative messages. The other half of you is struggling with the critical side. It's trying to push forward. But the self-saboteur in you is trying to drag you down and put you back in your place. We all do these kinds of things to stay emotionally safe. Our early experiences in life shape this voice, and that may help explain why it is the way it is. Your environment also plays a role. If you are lonely, unhappy, and feel uncomfortable, then this will play a part in shaping how you talk to yourself. You need help to stop this behavior. Are you denying yourself because you don't believe that you deserve more than what you have now?

Mess up #7: fear. Holding ourselves back because we are afraid of change.

This is one of the most common reasons why we deny ourselves. We are afraid of failure, afraid that our anti-self will succeed in rising against us. Rejection doesn't feel good, and failure sucks. However, you are far more resilient than you believe you are. The voice whispering in your ear, telling you that you're capable, is the same voice that is feeding your fear. The reality of life is that it is painful and it is joyful. The more you live and love, the more likely you are to experience the pain. When you deny yourself the pursuit of what you can achieve, you're robbing yourself of the joy.

Mess up #8: Rigidity.

Holding on to the negative self-image of yourself is destructive. Sadly, we rarely challenge that negative view of ourselves because we're used to it. Since it's familiar, it's comfortable. You make the rules based on those lies, and you believe that you're protecting yourself.

Did you get shouted at a lot as a child if you got too loud? Keeping quiet prevented that shout, yet if you act timidly as an adult, you are denying yourself opportunity.

Did you lose your temper in a bid to get attention from your parents? It worked then. But doing that in an adult relationship will push people away. We formed fences to protect ourselves, but they don't translate from childhood to adulthood. We must adapt and move forward.

Mess up #9: Believing you can master the "how" without a "who" to teach you the "how."

You cannot hold yourself accountable. You will always run into some obstacle. Realize that, without accountability, your progress can slow to a stop. As I'm writing this book, I am being held accountable to an accountability coach, who makes me get it done. And, of course, I wait till the last session. But guess what? You're reading this book because somebody else held me accountable to finish. Make sure that you do yourself a favor and get somebody to hold you accountable.

Mess up #10: Super Soul Sunday Syndrome.

What is Super Soul Sunday Syndrome? This refers to that Oprah show, *Super Soul Sunday*. When we watched that show, we felt good by the end and motivated by it. We fooled ourselves into believing that the good feeling meant that we'd changed, but we were only entertained.

You may be having that feeling right now. You feel on top of the world because this book was entertaining. But it's not going to be transformative unless you do something with what you read to create real change.

My hope for you is that you do something. Now, you can do this something all by yourself, but that would be the slow way. You're going to run into obstacles that you didn't expect. You could stop and be stuck here for *years* without answers. Let's face it, you've got this far into this book because all you know, with all your education and brilliance, hasn't solved the problem of you getting what you want, which is to be respected and appreciated.

This is the time for you to be really honest (this is the "R" in the process, to reflect and take radical responsibility) and decide either to keep banging up against the way ...

... or you can take the quick way out and hire a coach or a mentor. I say *hire* because when you pay, you pay attention. When you've paid someone, they will give you 100 percent of their focus to make sure you achieve what you set out to achieve.

Are you going to do this the easy way and hire a coach? Or are you going to do this the hard way and think that you can figure it out on your own?

If you could figure it out on your own, you wouldn't have needed to read this book; in fact, you likely wouldn't even have picked it up.

Your first task is to admit that you don't know how to get respect. Just because you read a book, it doesn't necessarily mean you know how to implement all the steps, or how to overcome all the obstacles you will come up against. Make sure you don't fall into Mess Up #1 above, by depending on your IQ and believing that you can do it on your own. Get a coach or a mentor on your team immediately. Yes, I would love to help you. Now is the time to reach out and ask.

12

THE SECRET TO HELPING YOURSELF

I'm romantic and I love those fairytale endings. You can have a fairytale ending. Here's what I want for Anna: I want Marcus to come back, and when Marcus comes back, I want him to realize that Anna is a unique, loving, beautiful, and giving jewel. She deserves to be treated like the precious jewel that she is—and that means listening to her, figuring out what she needs, not just what he needs. I want a wedding. I want the doves flying in the air. I want to see her wearing white, walking down the aisle. My desire for Anna and Marcus is to be together. Because Anna loves Marcus a lot.

But I have a condition to that story. Anna must do the work on realizing her value and understanding her Human Design and her spirit.

It's my hope that, after going through the steps, and with months of working through the tears, anger, and pain, wondering why it had to be this way, Anna will change her energy to a level of respecting herself. When Marcus returns, Anna will understand that he can't be the same as he was before because it's not going to work. Anna will have changed into a self-respecting woman. As she realizes her needs, Marcus will be able to see that.

Dr. Sydney is well on her path, and her next step is figuring out how to do exactly what she wants to do in her career. Working together, we have gone through the steps of this journey, of The R.E.S.P.E.C.T Method™. She has embraced her changed life in only ten weeks' time, and now she has a way to bring her unique heart to the world and an offer for compensation.

If you haven't read my book *Too Smart to Be Struggling*, you may want to pick that up. Although I wrote the book for my doctor colleagues, it has ended up being extraordinarily valuable for people who aren't physicians, but for those who want to figure out, "How do I get from where I am, to being able to change, and changing and creating a new career."

Working with Dr. Sydney, I realized that the most valuable sessions were about knowing who she is and respecting herself. That led me to this book and taking you through these steps. Both Dr. Sydney and Anna are well on their way to a better place as they continue to perfect the steps in their life that relate to The R.E.S.P.E.C.T. Method. It's my sincere desire that you're able to go through these steps, too, and perfect them.

If you've got this far in this book, I know you're interested in seeing true transformation in your life. You want to solve the problem of being underappreciated and not getting the respect you want. My wish for you is that you are able to do that fully, enjoy your life, and get the appreciation that you deserve.

This isn't just another good book to go on your shelf and talk about on Zoom or at a party. You need to do something besides writing a list and making vision boards. You will need to invest in your spiritual self.

In fact, you're going to need to tithe to yourself. What does that mean? Tithing is the concept of giving 10 percent. It is not just donating 10 percent of your money, but also 10 percent of your time and your talent.

What type of spiritual growth could be realized? And what type of life would you have, if you tithed 10 percent of your time, your talent, and your money to yourself? And when is the last time you did that, or have you *ever* invested 10 percent of everything you have into your own growth?

I hope that, after reading this book, you understand that you deserve it. But it's not going to just happen from reading. You must be willing to make the *energetic* exchange. You give, and then you get. That's the concept of "give, and it shall be given unto you." You make the investment, and the universe will give you back even more than you invest.

Learn how to use your unique spiritual DNA and develop and use your spiritual intelligence and quotient. By doing this, you're going to be the authentic You, and you will get the respect and appreciation you deserve. That's important. You need to be held accountable by someone other than yourself. It is necessary for you to commit to investing in somebody to help you do that.

Life's struggles serve to move us along on our journey. Struggles are an opportunity for growth, and, at any one time, you can struggle in one of the five areas of your life—health, money, relationships, career or purpose, and spirituality and personal groups. Struggles don't simply go away from thinking excessively about them or analyzing or making lists.

If you are thinking excessively about your struggles, that is what I refer to as a block or, in plain terms, an obstacle. Which area of your life do you need help with right now? What is your biggest obstacle? Are you self-aware enough to admit and accept and receive help?

This book is written for you. If you're serious, then now is the time to understand that whining and complaining doesn't work. You're finally ready to take action and receive help, because that is how you will overcome obstacles. You have a unique success code that you were born with. Do you know how to read it? Once you know how to read your success code, and learn to follow it to a tee, life will seem to flow like a river, without you always feeling like you're swimming against the flow.

One of the secrets to fast-track your development is to bring in a mentor. Mentors are an incredible resource in the pursuit of development. Mentors generally are experts in their sphere of influence, but, at a minimum, they are people more knowledgeable and experienced than you in a particular area. Mentors add value because they lead and guide you as you pursue information and challenge yourself. Having traveled a similar path to obtain their current level of mastery, they know the challenges to be faced and the pitfalls to avoid. Having a mentor to consult, to help you think and work through challenges, ultimately ensures that you stay on the right track toward meeting your outlined goals and expanding your understanding.

Are you ready to overcome the challenges in your life, be held accountable, and learn how to put all the information you are reading about into actions that work to help you reliably reach your goals? You know what you need to do, but you just can't seem to make yourself do it or stick to it. Or you may be one of the brave souls who admit that they don't know what to do, or don't even know what to ask for, but they know they need to do something different.

One thing is for certain, blocks are unlikely to go away on their own. It's your responsibility to deal with them if you wish to have more of everything in life, including respect and appreciation. Coaching and mentorship exist to help you identify exactly where you are, to help you figure out specifically how to get where you want to be.

If you finish this book and know exactly what to do, go do it. There are two ways you can do this. There's the easy way, and there's the hard way. The hard way is figuring it out on your own, looking at the steps and slowly crawling along, like a blind snail, with no guidance. The easy way is to immediately invest in coaching and mentoring.

I'd love to help you do that. If that's something that you are interested in, you can get started at drveronica.as.me/getrespect, where you'll be able to fast-pace your transformation.

When you run into an obstacle, you'll have someone to help you determine what that obstacle or block is, and you can cocreate a solution quickly and in real time. My goal for you is that you move forward and live your life purpose, and that you are on your master path. I'm so grateful that you decided to take the time to read this far, and I wish you all the success in the world.

It's easy to see the people you feel are not giving you respect as the villains in your story. When you read my story about what happened in my marriage, it's being told from my perspective. I made a point to say he's a nice guy. You probably still don't believe that, because the way we live our life is by opposites—good, bad, up, down, villain, heroine. I am the heroine of my story. And I'm writing it from the perspective of being a heroine.

But what's deep down is this. If you were to ask my former husband if he respected me when we were in our relationship, he would say, "I respect Veronica. She's a great person. She's brilliant. She's beautiful. And she's a great wife." He would say that he never disrespected me until, of course, the end, when everything got contentious, as things do at the end of relationships. We were both responsible for how things ended.

When people aren't respecting you, many times, they're not even aware of it. What about those abusive relationships where it's clear to everyone, including both people in the relationship, that there's no respect going on? If you're in that type of situation, I get it. It's easy to see. But there are so many of us who are in situations where it's not so clear. But there's something about the energy of the relationship that makes it obvious to other people that something is not quite right.

I've had more than one friend mention to me, "I don't think he appreciates you properly." It might have been the tone of his voice when he answered me. It might have been in the way he phrased something that seemed dismissive. I shrunk back under these circumstances.

I've seen many strong women do the same in their romantic relationships. They stay because they believe that's what they're supposed to do, or that's just the way relationships are. Nobody's perfect. I'm not perfect, he's not perfect. We're doing the best we can.

From the outside, people can tell that you're not getting the appreciation and respect that you deserve. From the inside, you know it, too.

This is the elephant in the room. It's hard for us to admit it, because when we do, it means we might have to do something about it. Doing something about it is scary because what does that mean? It means, probably, creating strife in the relationship.

Can a relationship with less respect than it deserves be repaired? Yes. However, both partners must agree that there is a problem in the relationship. They then must also enlist the help of an objective training professional to help work through the issues. It requires both people in the relationship to decide that there's something that they are not happy with in themselves, that they want to improve as an individual, for themselves and for the relationship.

If I had to pick the number one reason that I decided my marriage was irreparable, what would I say? I'd say it was because, when it was time for us to go to counseling, my soon-to-be ex-husband had already decided that the whole problem in the relationship was me and not him.

There are two people in a relationship. If they want it to work, both must agree to listen to each other and be willing to make some changes. I also decided to leave because I read a book called *Real Love* by Greg Baer, MD. The line I remember best from this book is, "if you're unhappy in a relationship, it's you." That's the problem. I took that to heart. I know that's the truth. If I'm unhappy, it's my problem to fix my unhappiness. It's no one else's problem. It's not about me changing other people. It's about me changing myself so that I feel content. That might mean that I need to choose to leave a relationship.

When you're in a marriage or long-term relationship, especially if you're in a marriage with children, it's challenging to convince yourself that things are so bad that you have to leave. Think about how true this rings in all relationships, even the ones where women are being beaten down and threatened. It's hard for them to decide that it's better to be outside the relationship when they are still inside. This happens because, when we're being treated the way we're being treated, we believe deep down that it's what we deserve. So, we take it. We allow someone else to punish us as a form of punishing ourselves.

When I decided that I had the courage to walk away, because there was something better out there for me that I deserved, I walked away.

That was a scary day. Walking away meant that I was giving up on my hopes and dreams. When we walk into a relationship, when we walk into a job, we have vast hopes and dreams for our future. When we give up on a particular situation, we feel like our hopes and dreams aren't going to come to fruition. Except the truth is, when you decide to walk away, and into a new situation, where you're appreciated for being the authentic You, where you don't have to fake, where you don't have to change yourself into something or somebody else, that's when your hopes and dreams flourish.

The same goes for professional and family situations. When you finally stand up for yourself in a well-thought-out way, the people who do respect you are going to come forward to help you and give you something better. When you stay in a job where you're being treated poorly, all the people around you are observing you being treated poorly. And guess what? In their mind, they're saying, "Well, that's what she thinks she's worth. So, why would I think she's worth more than that?" You won't be considered for promotions and new positions.

By being the nice girl who shuts up and says nothing, what generally happens under these circumstances is that a less qualified man comes in and takes the position that she's been wanting for years. When you sit back, and you are quiet and nice, and you just smile sweetly, that's a sign to people that you're not qualified enough. You have to assert yourself.

Asserting yourself doesn't mean you're a bitch, although some people might call you that. In your quest to never be called a bitch, you have sabotaged yourself. You know that when somebody calls you a bitch, you're probably being the right amount of assertive.

There's going to be people out there that simply see you for who you are, as someone who stands up for their beliefs and gets what they deserve. But there will always be haters who will try to tear you down. You will need to put those people in their place, by being well-prepared and strong, continuing to be your true self, and not allowing yourself to be intimidated.

Your goal is to gain the courage to do what you know you must do, in order to get the respect and appreciation that you deserve in life. Sometimes that means making difficult choices, like leaving a job or leaving a relationship.

How badly do you want your life to be the way you want it? Or would you rather be living it subpar, the way somebody else thinks that you should live?

The way to take charge of your life is to *take charge of your life!* Do not let anyone else, including the boss or the spouse or the lover, make decisions for how things are going to go for you.

ABOUT THE AUTHOR

Psychic Intuitive Guide and Relationship Coach Dr. Veronica Anderson is the bestselling author of 4 books including *"Get the Respect You Deserve: 7 Secrets to Getting Seen and Heard in Your Job and Relationships."* Dr. Veronica transitioned from her own private practice as an Eye Surgeon to a Spiritual Guide & Transformational Coach delivering individual and group programs to help her clients overcome strange, rare, and peculiar issues. Using her skills as intuitive and her signature R.E.S.P.E.C.T Method, Dr. Veronica guides high-achieving professional women on how to make successful career, health, and relationship transitions by learning the process to become their beautiful authentic selves. She uses tools such as Psychic Intuitive Energy Readings, the Kolbe Assessment, and Human Design to help people deeply understand their spiritual nature, instincts, and intuition and how to use them to get what they want in their career and in romance..

Dr. Veronica Anderson began her medical career as an Eye Surgeon after graduating from Princeton University and Rutgers Medical School (with honors) and now has the distinction of being both a licensed physician and a practicing psychic. Dr. Veronica is an Integrative Medicine Physician, certified in Functional Medicine and trained in Homeopathy.

In her programs, Dr. Veronica uses her gifts and talents to help people with strange, rare, and peculiar issues who feel like they just haven't gotten answers or results from strategies they have tried previously. She provides guidance to her clients who receive clarity, validation, and confirmation which decreases fear and increases confidence.

Dr. Veronica hosted her on podcast and AM radio show for several years and has appeared in national television as well as multiple syndicated radio shows and podcasts. She is a 3rd Degree Black Belt in Tae Kwon Do who splits her time living in Bucks County, Pennsylvania, Harlem, New York City, and Nice, France with her husband and two dogs, Artemis and Apollo.

Made in the USA
Middletown, DE
22 February 2023